Bob Paisley

Bob Paisley

A Lifetime in Football

ARTHUR BARKER LIMITED LONDON
A subsidiary of Weidenfeld (Publishers) Limited

Published in Great Britain by
Arthur Barker Ltd
91 Clapham High Street
London SW4 7TA

ISBN 0 213 16767 0

Printed in Great Britain by
Butler & Tanner Ltd
Frome and London

Contents

Acknowledgements

There are many people who have helped me in the production of this book with their advice and encouragement, and my thanks go to them all.

In particular I would like to thank Derek Doyle for his help in getting the book published, John Keith of the *Daily Express*, Colin Wood of the *Daily Mail*, Chris James of the *Daily Mirror* and Mike Ellis of the *Sun* for supplying me with dates and facts and figures that even I had forgotten.

I would also like to thank the people not directly involved in this book, the directors and staff of Liverpool FC, and the late Bill Shankly, and the best fans in the world - Liverpool supporters.

And lastly my thanks go to my wife and children, who have been through it all with me.

Picture Acknowledgements

The photographs in this book are reproduced by kind permission of the following:

Anpfoto, Central Press Photos, County Press Wigan, *Daily Express, Daily Mail, Daily Mirror, Daily Star, Evening Standard*, Alain Gassmann, *Liverpool Daily Post and Echo*, Newspix, Harry Ormesher, Photeck, Larry Sayle, *Sun, Sunday Express, Sunday Mirror*.

1 From Bricks to Bullets

My first glimpse of Rome in 1944 was through the dusty windscreen of a 15cwt army truck. My second visit was rather different – as manager of the Liverpool side which won the European Cup for the first time.

No wonder it's known as the Eternal City. That's exactly how it will be remembered by the thousands of Liverpool fans who also invaded it to witness a unique occasion.

But Gunner Paisley of the Royal Artillery was not to know that when we passed through after fighting our way up the heel of Italy. Football was the last thing on my mind then. Survival was the name of the game. I didn't even know if there would be any football to come home to. My career as a professional with Liverpool had lasted just three months when I was called up. Anfield was only a pleasant memory for a young hopeful who had signed on in May 1939.

I had played only two reserve team games when the army beckoned, but by then I had already met and been deeply impressed by a young man who was already Liverpool's first-team captain – a certain Matt Busby. A lifetime's friendship and respect for the man was born then and has survived ever since.

But I'm breaking one of Liverpool's golden rules by racing ahead of myself. We believe in organisation at Anfield and keeping everything as simple as possible. It's a good habit, so I shall start at the beginning....

Hetton le Hole is a typical Durham mining village, a close-knit community seven miles from Sunderland where coal was king and football was a religion. My father was a miner, and although he never wanted any of his four sons to go down the pit, there didn't seem to be many alternatives. We lived in a small terraced house, and although we never went short of life's essentials, there was never much money left over by the end of the week.

There are many similar villages dotted all around the North-East, and working-class lads automatically turned to football, not just as a recreation, but as a way of life. I was particularly fortunate in that my school, Eppleton Senior Mixed, was years ahead of its time where football was concerned. It was considered normal routine for a thirteen-year-old to be called out of class for his regular egg and sherry tonic when there was a big cup-tie coming up. And there were plenty of them too. We were usually competing for six trophies every season, and if we didn't win them there was something wrong.

Every pupil was expected to contribute sixpence a season towards maintaining the football team. For that they were promised a place at every home game and the side was kitted out with boots and balls supplied by the local Co-op. If ever a school team was run on professional lines it was Eppleton, and for someone like me who was going to make soccer his career, it was a priceless introduction.

The school caretaker, Bowler Burns, would provide mustard baths in the boiler house; the sportsmasters, Bertie Rowe, Jimmy Johnson and Alec Wright, supervised the running and organisation of the team, and if we were not playing for the school there were always impromptu training sessions. We couldn't afford to buy our own football, but I had an uncle who worked in the Co-op slaughterhouse and many a time we improvised with a pig's bladder on some unsuspecting farmer's field or just in the street.

The North-East is a world of its own. In those days there were no motorways, and this encouraged the feeling that we were a little slice of England totally independent from the rest. The big cities in the South might as well have been in another country. Football centred on Durham and Northumberland – a match at Whitley Bay was really going to the outer limits.

By the time I was fourteen, I had signed for Wolves on

schoolboy forms, but they wanted to delay a decision about taking me to Molineux. I couldn't wait. It was time to start earning my living and I followed my father to the pit. But three months after I had started, he was badly injured in an accident underground and didn't work again for five years. I will never forget that day. I knew instinctively who was on the stretcher when they brought him out. It was a bad time. Modern methods were being introduced to mining and some of the old shafts were in a dangerous condition.

Ironically the Hetton pit was closed soon afterwards and I was out of a job. But I was lucky. A pal of mine was a footrunner who had won three big handicap races in the area. There was big betting on these events and some local builders had won a nice pile backing my pal. He was out of work too, but on the strength of their winnings the builders offered him a job as an apprentice bricklayer, and there was a chance for me too.

Every day we would cycle nine miles to work and nine miles back, but there was still time to play football, and by this time I had joined Hetton Juniors. The cycling was to come in handy years later, too. I once pedalled it to Anfield from Tarporley in Cheshire to play in a reserve 'derby' match against Everton, and then cycled back to my army camp – a small matter of some fifty miles!

My big break came when the kings of amateur football, Bishop Auckland, signed me. I had two wonderful seasons with them, climaxed by winning the Amateur Cup at Roker Park when we beat Willington 3–0 after extra time. It was a great experience for an eighteen-year-old. Bishop Auckland became the first amateur side to win ten championships, just as Liverpool did years later at professional level.

Liverpool came along in May 1939, and although I had never even been to that side of the country, I jumped at the chance of joining them. Pre-season training did not begin until July, so they allowed me to complete the amateur season with Bishop Auckland – there was just the small matter of squeezing in another eleven games in a fortnight. One of them was against South Shields, a professional team, and we beat them too in yet another cup final.

When I eventually got to Anfield, I was a little boy lost. I remember the circumstances because they still apply today when a youngster joins a big club in a different part of the country. I only have to put him in my shoes to appreciate what a traumatic change it can be, especially if he has not been in a big city before. I am sure it's one reason why some talented youngsters don't make the grade. It is not a question of ability – it is all to do with adapting to new surroundings. As a manager, I am aware of this when a new boy comes to Anfield. It is important that they have someone to talk to. I was lucky, I could go to Matt Busby.

Joining the army was another big step. I was stationed in Rhyl in North Wales before setting sail for Egypt in 1941. It was a ten-week trip via the Cape and South Africa because it was impossible to go through the Mediterranean. We left in August, and by the time we had made camp south of Cairo, months had elapsed without any mail arriving. Every day I checked at the mail office to see if there was anything for me, and finally, in November, I got some reward. There were two sackfuls for my unit, and I was so pleased that I carried the lot back, convinced there would be a stack for me.

Instead, there was just one postcard from the Liverpool manager, George Kay, informing me that I had been selected for a Central League game at Preston at the beginning of August! The card had been sent to my old camp at Rhyl and had then taken another three months to reach me in Egypt. When I wrote back to Mr Kay, pointing out my whereabouts, he replied saying how lucky I was and how he wished he could change places with me. I felt the same way, wishing I could change places with him!

It was during the Western Desert campaign that I earned the nickname 'Gunner', and it's stuck ever since, although I can think of a few Liverpool players who have, over the years, called me a Desert Rat, often with the first word deleted.

The army showed me a big slice of the world and as a character-builder there is nothing quite like it. In common with most old soldiers I look back on that time with some affection. I am sure most of us remember only the good times, which is why, with hindsight, it all seemed very exciting. But I saw enough sand to last me a lifetime. That probably explains why I am happier now spending my holidays inland. I liked to go to see an old pal, Frankie Carr, at his racing stables in North Yorkshire, before he moved to Hong Kong, and now I visit Frankie Durr.

Rome, the first time, was just another stop on the way home, but further up Italy, in Florence, we used the soccer stadium as a camp and it was there I saw the great Joe Louis and Sugar Ray Robinson in the ring. The Americans had arranged for several world champions to fight exhibitions against the army's best, and the great Joe Louis was one of them.

This particular day, Louis was paired with a giant of a bloke. There was no sign of Louis when the army's big hope climbed into the ring, and the longer he had to wait, the more agitated he became. When Louis, sporting a spreading waistline which suggested he was hardly in peak condition, finally made his appearance, his opponent had had time to work himself into a real old lather.

When the bout began, he swarmed all over Louis, who was content to block everything, until one or two punches found their target. Louis signalled to the army corner, presumably to tell them to get their man to ease off as he did not want to hurt the guy. Unfortunately, the GI got the wrong idea and thought he had Louis in trouble - with disastrous consequences. He went for the kill, dreaming, no doubt, of making himself an overnight sensation. Well, he was certainly dreaming a few seconds later!

Louis' fist hardly moved as he connected. The soldier's gumshield flew out of his mouth as he hit the canvas and Louis just turned his back and ambled to his corner - he knew it was a KO without even looking. The whole fight has lasted less than four minutes, and Louis had thrown only one punch. It is not generally known that Louis, in fact, signed professional forms for Liverpool while on a promotional tour of Britain, but they were never forwarded to the Football League.

I have always been interested in boxing, and watching one of the all-time greats in action many years ago certainly whetted my appetite. That's why, in later years, it was a pleasure to see some of the big names at close quarters at Anfield.

We have always allowed sportsmen from all walks of life to use our medical rooms and I have had the privilege of attending a number of world champions over the years, including John Conteh, Hogan Kid Bassey and Alan Rudkin.

Conteh used to come to me as an amateur when he lived at Kirkby. Usually he was troubled by hand injuries even at that stage of his career. Yet, ten years on, he was still fighting in world championship bouts. Brittle hands are the biggest handicap any fighter can have, and although John may not be remembered as a great world champion, I suspect that the people who worked closely with him could tell another story. When you consider how much pain he must have endured with those suspect hands, I think his achievements have been quite remarkable.

But boxing was forgotten when we eventually came home – for even Woolwich seemed like home after over four years abroad. And it had happy memories for me too. It was on a trip back there after playing a match in the north of England that I met my wife.

She was sitting in the railway compartment when I accidently dropped my kit-bag on her sandwiches. It was quite an original approach, you must admit, especially as I would never normally win prizes for speaking to strangers.

Football was slowly getting under way again, with regional leagues all over the country. It was pretty haphazard, because so many of the players were still miles away from their clubs. Anyone could play for whichever team happened to be nearest. I remember the great Peter Doherty being spotted in the grandstand at Blackpool just before kick-off and being hurriedly directed to the dressing-rooms to wear the tangerine shirt. There was disappointment for some youngster stripped and ready to play, but I would have been proud any time to be able to say that Peter Doherty wore my shirt!

Being stationed at Woolwich and trying whenever possible to get to Merseyside to play, presented its problems. If I was due some leave, I would get a pass made out to Durham, and head straight for Merseyside. At the station I would tell the ticket collector I was just breaking my journey and do the same when I set off from Liverpool for the North-East after the game.

On one occasion a leave pass took me from Woolwich to Liverpool, on home to Durham and back up to Bradford for another game, return to Durham and eventually back to Woolwich. All highly illegal, of course, but then I was only breaking my journey, wasn't I?

Looking back, the war cost me six years of my playing career, but it was a time when there was no other choice. Many young professionals had to pick up the pieces like me, but we were the lucky ones - some never even had that option in 1945.

2 The Championship Business

If you look up any football records book and study the list of League championship winners, you will see that Liverpool led the way with 13 titles after our success in 1982, followed by Arsenal with eight. It was my ninth – and I was still looking for another.

I point out that fact, not to be big-headed, but because of the tremendous pride I feel in having collected more First Division championship medals than any other individual in the history of the game in this country. Anyway, it would be foolish to boast about it on a personal level because winning the hardest league in the world can be achieved only by total team effort – not only by the players on the field, but by the manager and backroom staff behind the scenes.

Unless everyone is rowing together the boat will soon wander off course, and from August to May is a long and testing voyage in all sorts of different weather conditions.

I won my first League medal as a player in the Liverpool team of 1946–47, the first season of organised football after the war, and my next two came when I was right-hand man to Bill Shankly in 1963–64 and 1965–66. Bill was still manager when I won my fourth medal with Liverpool in 1972–73, and after that I succeeded him and won five championships in seven seasons between 1976 and 1982.

If anyone had predicted that little lot when I joined the club as a teenage wing-half from the North-East on 8 May 1939, I would have just laughed at them. Even now it seems hard to believe.

Football has changed dramatically since my playing days and what it takes to win championships has changed with it. The demands made on players today are enormous compared to the 1940s and 1950s when English clubs did not compete in European competitions and there was no League Cup.

In my day, if you played forty-eight matches a season you could win everything that was open to you – namely the League and the FA Cup. In fact, we almost landed the 'double' in 1947, but lost 1–0 in a semi-final replay to Burnley at Maine Road.

Contrast that with the cluttered programme of today, when the League Cup is compulsory and the challenge of European football is irresistible, not only from the prestige point of view but for financial reasons also. If you have a run in the cup competitions you find yourself ploughing through a staggering amount of games in a season, and if one of them happens to be a European tournament there is the important but often overlooked factor of air travel to contend with – a subject I will discuss in detail in the *Mind and Body* chapter.

It is no mean feat to win a championship when you are battling on the European front as well – and Liverpool have been doing that without a break since 1964 and have gone on regularly winning titles. That means an average of about sixty games a season, and international players can face as many as seventy matches when you include tours that can leave them with as little as three weeks' break from football during the summer.

International duty can also affect players mentally. It can turn them over emotionally because of worries about whether they are going to be selected in the first place and, if they are, whether they play well enough to be chosen again. Liverpool have had as many as ten players away for their countries during international weeks, and all you can do then is hope they don't suffer injury and that they report back physically and mentally in tune for the next club match.

While clubs have learned to live with these demands, it remains a fact that when a player's regular routine of training and match preparation is disturbed, then the outcome is in the lap of the gods. With so many unknown factors always liable to hit you during the course of a season, it is essential that the planning and preparation is solid. At Liverpool we start working on that in the summer, before a ball is even kicked. When the season's fixtures are published they are gone through with a fine-tooth comb. Dates, travelling distances, opposition and other relevant details are carefully noted.

If there is a period that is likely to make heavy demands on the team, the club's general secretary, Peter Robinson, will go into action to try to re-arrange dates of fixtures. The games in question may be six or seven months hence, but you can't leave anything to chance. You have enough of the unexpected to contend with as it is. Doing it this way, anticipating problems before they arise, is not breaking any rules or regulations. It is not taking advantage of anybody. It is simply asking for co-operation from another club – and they always have the right to refuse.

The late summer, of course, is the dawn of the new season. But at Liverpool we realise that the programme stretching ahead is a marathon. And the knowledge acquired from years of experience is reflected in the training programme. If you are running in a marathon you have to train for one, and our programme is devised to build players gradually to a mental and physical peak, so that in the middle of the season they are ticking over like a well-oiled and run-in car. Then it becomes a case of keeping them topped up from a fitness point of view, and when you are involved in midweek matches the games themselves provide this.

As soon as possible in the early stages of the season the players have their anti-flu and tetanus jabs. Not only are they then protected for the season ahead but the effect of any reaction they might suffer is kept to a minimum.

Training has been revolutionised since the days when I was a player. We had no training ground then. We just ran around the Anfield track and managed to get on the pitch only in the early season when the ground was dry.

Today, of course, Liverpool boast a superb training centre called Melwood in the city's suburbs, and modern players see far more of the ball in training than we did. Our programme at Melwood has been one of the rocks on which Liverpool's consistency has been built, and both Bill Shankly and I always attached tremendous importance to our work there.

Unlike at some clubs, all the training is done there and Anfield is kept for matches only. I would like to see this happen at every club, and I strongly believe that nobody should be allowed to train on a pitch the day before a match. When cash grants are being handed out to football clubs this should be made a priority and clubs who do not have adequate facilities should be helped to acquire them.

The playing surface is such a major factor in performance that it is essential we give more thought to the care and maintenance of pitches. Liverpool have been blessed with excellent ground staff, and Anfield's head groundsman, Arthur Riley, spent an amazing fifty-four years in the service of the club until his retirement in 1982. The changes he has seen have been many and varied, but he singled out sand-slitting of pitches as the finest development of all. It promotes drainage and growth, and the results are superb.

Unfortunately, Arthur's last season in charge at Anfield coincided with the worst pitch problems we have ever known at the club following the laying of undersoil heating in the summer of 1980. The state of the pitch during the 1981–82 season was no reflection on Arthur, our stadium manager Bert Johnson or any of the Anfield staff. The problem was soil compaction and a condition known as 'thatching', and I'm convinced we were let down by the experts when our under-pitch heating was installed.

It took Everton three attempts over the years at laying various forms of undersoil heating before they got it right, and I believe Liverpool's first attempt rebounded on us. In my view, although the pitch problems might not be directly attributable to the heating installation, the soil specialists should have been aware of the possible dangers and alerted us to them.

As it turned out the eventual state of the pitch provided us with a handicap at home right through the 1981–82 season – so, I trust, satisfying those people who have on several occasions made the ridiculous suggestion that Liverpool should be officially handicapped in the League to give other clubs a chance. Apart from the fact that such a notion is just nonsense, that sort of talk can get into the minds of referees and might just sway decisions against you in matches.

The headaches our pitch caused us during 1981–82 are reflected in the contrast between our home and away results. If we had produced anything like our usual quota of home wins we would have had the League championship wrapped up long before the end of the season.

I didn't make an issue of it at the time because I couldn't risk giving the players a mental block about the pitch, which we dyed green in places at one stage just to improve its appearance.

You might trot out to me the old cliche that 'a pitch is the same for both sides'. I have never gone along with that completely, because put Liverpool on a good surface and we are as good as anybody and better than most at knocking the ball around, one-touch style. But the state of our pitch distracted our players and they lost a bit of confidence through it.

The reason I attach so much importance to the state of pitches is because a good surface encourages good football and allows skill to make its impact. And without skill you will never win a championship. On a mudheap even a skilful side can get bogged down, and then the match becomes a lottery. Many of the so-called FA Cup 'shocks' happen for this very reason.

Even at Melwood, Liverpool have always reserved one pitch for matches only, with the rest of our training work done on other areas of the ground, and, just as Arthur over the years maintained a fine playing surface at Anfield, the Melwood head groundsman, Eli Wass, has done likewise at the training ground.

It is because of the quality of their pitches that Liverpool have developed the tried and trusted habit of choosing countries like West Germany and Holland for pre-season matches. The surfaces there invite you to play football. It breeds confidence in players when they can knock the ball around accurately, and when a side is doing that it also develops teamwork.

Pre-season games are conditioners to the testing programme ahead. The games have to be teethy enough without being over-competitive, and travelling abroad for them builds the club spirit, helps players become mentally as well as physically attuned, and gives them a change of environment and routine from the training programme.

So many people have asked what has been the secret of Liverpool's unprecedented success. There isn't one, except that we acknowledge you can never stop learning and putting it to good use.

In the filing cabinet of my Anfield office I have built up a collection of desk diaries for each season in which all sorts of details were noted, ranging from weather conditions for a match in September to the fact that a certain player was late for training on a day in March. Nothing can be discounted as unimportant. But as I said earlier, no one man sitting in the manager's seat can successfully run a club like Liverpool. It has to be a team effort on and off the field, and the backroom staff are key men. When you have to contend with so many factors such as training, travel, hotels, food and the like, their foresight to sniff out any problems before they arise is absolutely vital.

The best planning and preparation in the world, of course, is useless without the raw material of the championship business – the players themselves. I have often been quoted as saying 'you can only play with what's available', and another comment of mine that has been printed time and time again is that 'Liverpool are a good team when they play well'.

What I am driving at is that a manager has to cut his coat according to his cloth – he has to mould his team's style of play to the players he has available. The same principle applies to the individual player. None of them is perfect, so you have to develop their stengths and cover or reduce their weaknesses. It is up to the manager to study players, to recognise certain factors in their playing ability as well as their characters and personal make-up.

Over the years I have struck up a firm friendship with racing trainer Frank Carr – the horses are my second sporting interest – and I have spent many a day in his yard at Malton in Yorkshire just looking at the animals being put through their paces. One thought has continually struck me – similarities to be seen between race horses and professional footballers. Some of the horses are frisky in the yard but might not do it on the track. Then there might be the one who steadily plods through training but can produce that extra sparkle on the day. In other words, they are all individuals. Players are no different, and it is the job of the manager and backroom staff to recognise their different personalities, their strengths and weaknesses, and plan accordingly. You delve into their backgrounds, their career histories and find out what makes them tick.

Apart from all the other problems I had to contend with so soon after succeeding Bill Shankly as manager, I was left with the legacy of harnessing Ray Kennedy's talents to Liverpool's pattern of play. He had made his name and reputation as an Arsenal front runner, partnering John Radford, and had helped the London club to win the 'double' in 1971 when they beat Liverpool after extra time in the FA Cup Final at Wembley.

He signed for Liverpool on the same July day in 1974 that Bill Shankly announced his retirement, and after an early spell alongside Phil Boersma in our attack, when Kevin Keegan was suspended, he lost his place when John Toshack came back into the side to partner Kevin. Ray had really lost his appetite for playing up front, but I learned that he had played midfield as a schoolboy. I think he was surprised I had found that out.

But that knowledge turned out to be a blessing for both Ray and the club. I had a talk with him and told him we would try him out in midfield in the reserves. The results exceeded our wildest expectations. Ray quickly blossomed in the role, made a first-team place his own and went on to play for England. When he signed for Liverpool the £200,000 fee was a club record, but he proved one of the greatest investments Liverpool ever made.

His contribution to Liverpool's achievements was enormous, and his consistency remarkable. So much so, in fact, that on the rare occasions he missed a match his absence was felt deeply, simply because he was a midfield powerhouse with tremendous vision and knowledge of the game.

At Arsenal they thought he couldn't play under fourteen stone, but he got down to twelve stone ten pounds and his performances provided the answer. For his frame it is surprising that he takes only a size 7½ shoe and, playing in midfield, he utilised his assets far more than he could have done up front. But his experience as a forward helped him enormously in tight, attacking situations.

He showed the ability to open up a game and give you the width of the park. When intercepting a loose ball he would invariably hit a telling pass – and running on to one himself he was as good as anyone I've seen. He was many people's choice as English football's player of the seventies. You can't quibble with his honours. Amongst them are four seasonal 'doubles' – he achieved the domestic 'double' with Arsenal, twice helped Liverpool win the League and a European trophy in the same season and then the League Cup and European Cup in 1980–81 – his last full season at Anfield. But, above all, you can't quibble with Ray's performances at Liverpool, which were a credit to him.

I wonder what would have happened to him, though, if he had never been switched to the midfield beat? That little bit of knowledge that came down the line from a North-East school teacher proved to be invaluable.

I had a lot of time and respect for Ray. With both of us being from the North-East we could talk to each other and we had a good rapport – something that is not too common between a manager and player.

It was probably our mutual understanding that smoothed us through Ray's departure to Swansea in January 1982. We had reached a point when both of us knew it was time for him to move on without either of us saying it in so many words and without ever having an argument.

Twice within three months earlier in the season Ray had been sent off – the first time for reacting to an incident with Aston Villa's Allan Evans at Anfield, and then for clashing with Arsenal's Peter Nicholas in a League Cup tie at Highbury.

I doubt if Ray had totted up two bookings at Liverpool before that, never mind two dismissals, so clearly there was something wrong. I am a firm believer that if a player suddenly starts retaliating he's got something on his mind . . . something is concerning him. And particularly in Ray's case because he was never a man to abuse his physical strength. If opponents had a go at him, Ray was the type who would just brush them off or push them aside in a legitimate manner.

His close friend Jimmy Case had been transferred to Brighton at the start of the 1981–82 season, with Mark Lawrenson coming in the opposite direction, and maybe that had affected Ray in some way. But, clearly, all was not as it should have been with him.

We had a good heart to heart talk, and although he admitted something was affecting him, he could not put his finger on it. He did not feel the same kind of urge in his game any more, there was some kind of frustration nagging at him, and perhaps the incessant pressures to win things at Liverpool had become too much for him.

He had been unable to get back into our first team following his second suspension – his last Liverpool appearance was in the world club championship game against Brazilian club Flamengo in Tokyo in mid-December – and young Ronnie Whelan had been blooded in his place.

The outcome of our talk was a mutual acceptance of the view that it would be better for Ray personally as well as the club if he tried to rekindle his career elsewhere. At first he had his eyes and his heart set on moving to his native North-East, and he had talks with Sunderland. Stoke also showed an interest, but Ray finally opted to join Swansea and swell John Toshack's ex-Merseyside colony in South Wales.

The fact that we understood each other so well made his departure far less painful than it might have been. Having to tell great players that they are past their best, or that it is time to move on, is the most unpopular job in management.

There is no pleasure in having to do it – it's almost being cruel to yourself – but it's a big part of what football is all about. I have been in that situation with men like Tommy Smith, Ian Callaghan, Chris Lawler, Emlyn Hughes, Larry Lloyd, Alec Lindsay, Brian Hall, Steve Heighway, Peter Cormack and many others. The one consolation is that those of them who have stayed in the game realise that it's part and parcel of being a manager and they have to do the same. Ray, of course, has accepted the new challenge of

Swansea whole-heartedly.

In my view he was one of Liverpool's greatest players and probably the most underrated. And at England level he was totally mis-used. He had so much control and was such a good shielder of a ball that an opponent virtually had to knock him over to take the ball off him. He had a great footballing brain, and his striker's instinct in the box never left him – he was as dangerous as anyone when he got in there. The way he read my thoughts, moved up from midfield into attack and scored the decisive goal in the 1981 European Cup semi-final return with Bayern Munich proved that.

We knew what his strengths were at Liverpool, things were built around him, and we played according to his abilities which were recognised throughout Europe – except in England. He never received the acclaim he deserved in this country and at international level England wrongly asked him to 'pick people up'.

That was something he never did with Liverpool. In fact you can count the number of times Liverpool have specifically man-marked any player over the years – Sammy Lee on Bayern's Paul Breitner and Ian Ross on Everton's Alan Ball are two of the very few examples.

Ray's positional play was outstanding, but you would never give him the job of chasing after an opponent or delegate him to a defensive chore as England did. Certainly he could close people down – but that is a positional thing. Eventually, he had his fill of international football and announced in a Sunday newspaper that he never wanted to play for England again. It was sad that it worked out that way.

But he did a great and valuable seven-year stint for Liverpool, and I admit there were times after he had left us that I wished I still had him around.

Whether or not the unique demands made on a Liverpool player had taken their toll of Ray Kennedy, I'm convinced they were a major factor in Ray Clemence's decision to ask for a move after fourteen years at Anfield. Sometimes players don't realise the pressures they are under – and Ray was under plenty when he was at Liverpool. Apart from the challenge of constantly trying to win things with the club he had the rivalry with Peter Shilton for the England job and the limelight trained on him because of his regular appearances on radio and television.

Then our signing of Bruce Grobbelaar from Vancouver White-caps was probably the last straw that pushed Ray to ask for a move. My plan was the tried and trusted one at Liverpool of grooming Bruce in the reserves for a couple of years as a gradual successor to Ray. But Bruce, never short on confidence, told Ray that he would have his place before the end of the season. It meant that Ray faced a battle he had never faced in his life before. He said to me, 'Who does this fellow think he is?'

Finally, he came to see me and said he wanted a transfer. It was granted – and at a bargain price – simply because of all that he had done for the club. But for his great service the fee would not have been a penny under £450,000 rather than the £300,000 Keith Burkinshaw paid to take him to Tottenham. It was washers for the best goalkeeper in the country who, even though he is well into his thirties, is fit enough to go on playing until he is forty.

The fact that Ray moved to White Hart Lane on the rebound from his situation at Anfield was probably the reason why he got off to a bad start at Tottenham. By his standards it was a worse beginning than Bruce Grobbelaar had with us when we had to throw him in the deep end of First Division football. At Liverpool, Ray read the players in front of him and reacted to them, rather than tell them what to do. But he started out at Tottenham doing the reverse of that. Possibly, because of his reputation, defenders were looking for instructions from him before he knew what they were capable and incapable of doing. In the end, of course, his natural goalkeeping ability saw him through, and in my opinion confirmed that he had the edge on Shilton, probably because leaving Liverpool had relaxed him just that little bit.

Liverpool's standards *are* sky-high and we know what we want from a player. Perhaps that is the reason why several players who have come to Liverpool have had to serve almost a second apprenticeship before adjusting to the demands of the club and the standards it pursues.

Clemence himself, the greatest goalkeeper I have seen, spent two and a half seasons in the reserves before displacing Tommy Lawrence, whose performances through the sixties played a major part in Liverpool's success at the time. Tommy earned the nickname of the 'sweeper keeper' because of his ability to perform almost as an extra defender when the situation required. And even today, when he is at the pinnacle of his profession, Ray will tell you that he learned a great deal from Tommy before perfecting the art himself.

Terry McDermott had to wait a while before coming to terms with life at Anfield. Then he became an England player. Alan Hansen had to do the same – and played for Scotland.

When we signed Avi Cohen from Israeli club Maccabi of Tel Aviv – Liverpool's first foreign 'import' – we had no doubts about his skill. But then we had to build on that by developing his stamina and getting him used to the contrasting conditions and pace of English football. Unfortunately he never quite made it with us and returned to Israel.

Certain players, of course, have been signed by Liverpool and commanded a regular first-team place immediately, or very shortly after their arrival. This happens either through circumstances – Phil Neal, who got an early first-team chance because of Alec Lindsay's injury, and Grobbelaar, because of Clemence's departure, are prime examples – or because the player has been signed to do a specific job. We bought Graeme Souness from Middlesbrough to bring a different dimension to our game. Ian Callaghan, a wonderful servant to Liverpool, a fine player and a great professional, was nearing the end of his distinguished career. Graeme was the man who succeeded him in midfield, and comparing the two is a classic example of different players having different strengths and weaknesses in their game.

Cally was an outstandingly mobile player, a great team man and a hard worker. When he switched from his early career as a winger to midfield he would go round the houses with the ball to give himself time to think before distributing it. Graeme, on the other hand, does not possess Cally's stamina nor his defensive qualities. But his vision allows him to fling out quick passes, both long and short, to develop moves earlier. Cally was one of the players around whom Liverpool's success was built. He was one of the marathon men who went on season after season rarely missing a match, like Chris Lawler, Tommy Smith, Emlyn Hughes, Ray Kennedy and Phil Neal. They are a rare breed, and it is that kind of consistency and durability which is essential to winning championships.

You need a squad of not less than sixteen players, with the key men playing in at least thirty-six of the forty-two League games. If you get hit at the wrong time with a crop of injuries in the wrong places, you can be in trouble. That is why it is essential that the players not only look after themselves off the field, in terms of their social life and their diets, but also control themselves from a disciplinary point of view in matches. If they are going to get themselves sent off or suspended then they might as well be injured.

That is an attitude that has been carefully nurtured at Anfield. It is something managers and players can control.

When we won the championship in 1965–66 – finishing six points ahead of Leeds with a total of sixty-one points – we used only fourteen players, which is the fewest in one season in League history. Even of those fourteen, Bobby Graham made only one appearance and Alf Arrowsmith three. But we had five ever-presents – Tommy Lawrence, Gerry Byrne, Ron Yeats, Ian Callaghan and Tommy Smith.

The championship-winning squad of 1947, in which I played, involved twenty-six players. But even then there was a nucleus of us who played the majority of games. Goalkeeper Cyril Sidlow made 34 appearances, right-back Ray Lambert 36, right-half Phil Taylor 35, myself 33, Billy Liddell played 34 games on the wing, and two other forwards, Albert Stubbins and Jack Balmer, made 36 and 39 appearances respectively.

Although you cannot legislate for injuries, you can do your best to avoid them. And Liverpool's approach and style in training and matches is geared to this end. We always aimed to cut out the desperate situations when players can get hurt so easily, and in this respect it has been an education to study the marathon men I referred to earlier. They have provided a fine example for youngsters to follow and learn from.

Chris Lawler was a classic example. His whole approach to playing the game and winning the ball was so completely balanced. You never saw Chris making last-minute dashes or wild lunges, and consequently his risk of being injured was greatly reduced. His style of play bred consistency, and the same applied to men like Portsmouth wing-half Jimmy Dickinson, Southampton winger Terry Paine, and Harold Bell, the long-serving Tranmere Rovers defender whose 595 League games included a record 401 consecutive appearances. You play with your brain as well as your feet, and all these long-distance merchants proved that conclusively.

In my lifetime of football experience with Liverpool, I have played with, treated, coached and managed a host of great players and it has always been a temptation for me - and others - to choose my best all-time team.

I now succumb to the temptation and commit this 4-2-4 line up to print: Ray Clemence; Phil Neal; Mark Lawrenson; Ron Yeats; Emlyn Hughes; Kenny Dalglish; Graham Souness; Ian Callaghan; Kevin Kegan; Roger Hunt; Billy Liddell. Sub.: Ian St John.

I exclude myself, although I would have liked to play in a team like that! But on reflection, it really is an impossible task to pick one side from so many great names from different championship-winning teams. What about the likes of Chris Lawler, Ray Kennedy, Tommy Smith, Albert Stubbins, Phil Thompson, Gordon Milne, Peter Thompson, Jack Balmer, Steve Heighway, Phil Taylor, Gerry Byrne, Willie Stevenson, David Johnson and so many more? I think you will sympathise with the headache such a task presents!

I certainly dismiss the theory that players of yesteryear are either better or worse than those of today. It goes back to the individual once again: some would be better players in the modern game, others might struggle. Billy Liddell, for example, would be a priceless front runner today. He was another marathon man, possessing stamina, strength, speed and a hammer of a shot in both feet.

However, when it comes to selecting the best of the Liverpool championship sides I have been associated with in one capacity or another, I have to give my vote to the record-breaking side of 1978–79. Winning the hardest league in the world is no mean achievement in itself. But to do it in the style that team did it and with the brand of football they produced was simply magnificent. They not only set a new points record of sixty-eight – under the old two points for a win system – but conceded a mere sixteen goals and scored eighty-five. It is going to take some team to equal or better that feat in one season.

We used only fifteen players that season. Just one more than the record low of fourteen back in 1966. And the appearance figures support my statement that a corps of regular players is vital. Ray Clemence, Phil Neal, Ray Kennedy, Kenny Dalglish were ever-presents, Graeme Souness missed just one match, Phil Thompson played in 39, and Jimmy Case and Alan Kennedy in 37. Of the rest, Alan Hansen and Terry McDermott made 34 appearances, David Johnson and Steve Heighway 26, Emlyn Hughes 16, David Fairclough 3, and Sammy Lee 1.

Not only did that squad produce the best sustained performances I have seen over a season, but they also had a sense of timing. They clinched the title by beating Aston Villa at Anfield on 8 May 1979 – the fortieth anniversary of the day I joined the club, back in 1939!

Having said that, the present side could even outstrip that one. That is the way things tend to happen at Liverpool. . . .

3 Shanks

Bill Shankly provided me with two of the biggest shocks of my life. The first was when he suddenly retired; the second, and greatest of all, was when he died.

I remember receiving the news in the very early hours of 29 September 1981, and feeling stunned. I had thought he was indestructible and would go on for ever. He was always so fit; he had been a fitness fanatic all his life. I just could not believe that only a few days after being taken into hospital he had suddenly gone from us.

The only time I really knew him to be ill was when he missed much of the pre-season training in 1970 with an infected foot. He was in Walton Hospital and had to take it easy for a while. Through his life I don't think he ever had a serious illness. He had knocks while he was playing, of course. He had a cartilage out at one stage. A few times at Liverpool he had injuries. He did his ankle once and was laid off for about three weeks. What upset the rest of us was that we had to miss our five-a-sides until he was fit again and ready to play.

That awful news about Bill's death came more than seven years after he shocked me and everyone else in football by resigning as manager of Liverpool Football Club. I remember the day of his announcement well, too – 12 July 1974.

I've asked myself many times why he did it, and I have to say that I really don't know the answer. I still wonder about it now. Did he want to become a director, and was he refused? I wouldn't know, and in any case there was nothing I could do on that score. Was it because he wanted to go out at the top? We had just won the FA Cup, a year after becoming the first English club to win a

European trophy, the UEFA Cup, and the League championship in the same season.

Was he worried about having another team to build? Tommy Smith had been relieved of the captaincy in that last season. Ian Callaghan was getting no younger. Both went on playing for us and were in the side that won the European Cup three years later, but at that time it looked as if there could be a problem replacing them. Chris Lawler was no longer a regular in the side. These were great players who had been groomed by him.

Or was it because it was getting too demanding for a man who had set such a high standard for himself and the club? Honestly, I don't know. The first I knew of it, like almost everyone else, was when Bill made that shock announcement. I knew there had been a few tiffs. Things do not always run smoothly, even at the most successful of clubs, and you certainly knew when Bill had had a tiff. There were often times when Bill threatened to pack it in, but when he finally did it was a complete surprise to me.

I didn't want his job. I even tried talking him into staying. I suggested that if he went away on a world cruise to recharge his batteries we could see if we could handle it together when he came back. But Bill just said he'd had enough, and that was that. The reason I didn't want the job was that I knew a lot of the problems that would arise.

The whole thing was going to be difficult. I knew in my own mind that there would be things I would have to combat. First of all there would be comparisons with Bill. His record was fantastic, and there were people who said it could never be matched. Then there was his knowledge linked with his enthusiasm for the game. I knew that this was going to be the biggest problem. When he retired, he was invited here, there and everywhere. Quite rightly, people wanted to honour him for what he had done. But I knew that one or two would try to exploit his generosity and his knowledge, and that the only sufferer would be me. He had a lot of experience - fifteen years at Liverpool - and when he gave some people at other clubs the benefit of it after he left us I felt I was on the wrong end of it.

I also knew that there was some rebuilding to be done, and

that's something that just cannot be done overnight. These were the types of problem I was confronted with. I wasn't being a coward, I was being a realist.

But I was given his job, and I knew that even if we had any success I would not get the credit for it. I had one object in view, and that was to stablise the position. The club had had enough of a shock with Bill retiring, and I had to try to ride it. I had a staff of men like myself – Joe Fagan, Ronnie Moran, Geoff Twentyman and Tom Saunders. We had a responsibility to try to make sure Bill's departure didn't upset things too much.

I know I've been criticised for some of the things that happened with regard to Bill afterwards. People have said that I drove him away from the club. The relationship certainly became uneasy for a while, and in the eyes of many I was the villain of the piece. But just as Bill had said, on the day he arrived from Huddersfield fifteen years earlier, 'I'm the boss now, and we'll do it my way,' I had to say the same thing. Because Bill had said he'd had enough I didn't want to involve him.

I look back on that first season as a manager and think that was probably my most successful one. We didn't win anything, we finished second in the League to Derby County and to many people that was failure by previous Liverpool standards. I blamed myself for the fact that we didn't do better. At the end of that season I said I'd been like an apprentice in the Derby, riding a fancied horse too wide at the bends. But in addition to all the other problems, we also had the problem of the situation with Bill.

At first, after he finished, he would come down to our training ground at Melwood. The players still called him Boss. It didn't bother me. I both expected and accepted it. Then there was a report in a Sunday paper after a game at Ipswich quoting me as saying that in Bill's days too I used to run the show. It was totally untrue. I hadn't said it.

Bill took offence. I apologised. He was still free to come to the training ground, but it was his decision not to come down anymore. Still in all this I feel we had a mutual respect for each other. In the end he acknowledged that what happened had been the right thing. There was no way that I would have driven Bill away from Liverpool.

But I have to explain my attitude to him in those early days after I took charge. Why didn't I use him as an adviser? I'll admit there were times, particularly in that first season, when I felt I needed advice. I had problems which I would have liked to talk over with him. But I thought to myself, no, he packed in because he said he'd had enough. I didn't want to give him these problems.

Also, I had to take into account the fact that it was Bill, a man I had come to know very well through fifteen years of working closely together. I knew it would be difficult for Bill to do anything but the top job in any club. If he advised you, you had to take his advice. Bill was a boss man – and I don't mean that in any derogatory sense. If he had been elected on to the board at Liverpool he would have wanted top position; wanted to be in charge. His word was law – and that's not advice. But that was his strength. That was why Liverpool were so successful during the fifteen years he was in charge.

It was a dilemma. I didn't want to involve him in my problems and I certainly didn't want to drive him away. I even asked him if he wanted to do any scouting for Liverpool. Then I welcomed it when other clubs came to him and asked for his help. There were lots of clubs and managers who thought they could get free knowledge and advice from him. Some of them were just using him. Bill would talk football to anybody, he'd give his advice to anybody. If I'm guilty of anything, I'm guilty of not doing more to discourage those people who were using him.

Among other things, as I've said, it added to my problems. The things that happened were disturbing and a little distressing. I knew that people were picking Bill's brain about Liverpool. They were trying to get his knowledge on the cheap – and he certainly had plenty of knowledge. At Anfield some found it hard to understand why Bill was telling other clubs how to play against us. But he was being exploited because he just lived for football. He was asked for his advice and he gave it because he loved to talk about football.

Really it was a few trying to get his knowledge on the cheap.

On the other hand, there were others who approached him from the best of motives. They were aware that he missed the involvement in the game. They also felt they could relax him by bringing him into things. But that in itself would be a problem because Bill would find it difficult to relax when he was involved in football.

Clubs by the minute, it seemed, wanted him to help them. I was pleased and proud, from my association with him, that they held him in such esteem. But at the same time I realised I was going to have to stand on my own two feet as the manager of Liverpool.

I took on the job of following a legend; a man who was quite unique. He was idolised by the supporters, probably more than any manager has ever been idolised. I was going out to work for them and there was no way, whatever happened, that I was going to take the credit, having taken over the team that had just won the FA Cup.

My attitude was that somebody had to be the buffer between the shock departure of Bill and the new figure who would come in eventually to take over. Bill's image had to be broken – just as in an earlier case the image of Sir Matt Busby had to be broken at Manchester United before the club became successful again. No disrespect to the men who had finished, the men who created the image, but I knew that other clubs had run into all sorts of trouble from this particular problem. I didn't want a situation like that at Liverpool.

Could I have done more? Could I have done something to maintain the old relationship with Bill without the football involvement? My answer to that is that the only time we saw each other during the fifteen years we worked together was when it had something to do with football. Mind you, that was seven days a week!

In all our time together, we missed only two Liverpool first-team games between us. The one he missed was in 1965 when we played Stockport at Anfield in the FA Cup. He went off to Germany to watch Cologne, our opponents in the European Cup. When he returned he asked the porter at the station before getting the train back to Liverpool if there had been any shock results the previous night. Yes, he was told, Peterborough had beaten Arsenal. Then he caught sight of a result in the paper ... Liverpool 1, Stockport County 1. 'What do you think that is if it isn't a shock?' he shouted.

We went on to survive that shock against the team who were then bottom of the Fouth Division, and beat Leeds at Wembley to carry off the FA Cup for the first time in the club's history. In the third round the following season, I missed our Anfield meeting with Chelsea and we were knocked out 2–1. The next game I missed was sixteen years later in April 1982 after Bill had died ... our home League game against West Brom which an attack of pleurisy prevented me attending.

Events after Bill retired put us on the same footing. Not that I'm saying who was as good as whom, or who was better or worse. But to walk out, as he did, and then for things to turn out as they did was enough to make the most placid man envious. He was the man who had started it all off and laid the foundations. He had to take a lot of the credit for what happened at Liverpool afterwards.

But on the other score, there is a bit of credit due to me and the staff, because we changed the whole team over. For instance, of the twelve players who created history by becoming the first British club to retain the European Cup with our win over Bruges at Wembley in 1978, only four, Ray Clemence, Emlyn Hughes, Phil Thompson and Steve Heighway, who came on as substitute, had played in the Liverpool first team under Bill. And re-building has continued over the years.

I know Bill would dearly have loved to win the European Cup. It was a tragedy that we didn't do it at the first attempt, our first season in Europe back in 1964–65. We were greenhorns then. We won the FA Cup for the first time in the club's history, then went out of the European Cup in a controversial semi-final against Inter Milan. I don't think we really got alerted to it until Celtic won it under Jock Stein in 1967.

I have dwelt mainly so far on those tricky months after Bill left. I can honestly say I don't know why he left and that perhaps he didn't know either. But there's no doubt that his arrival from

Huddersfield in December 1959 was the wind of change that blew through Anfield and revived the whole set-up.

I played against Bill when he was coming to the end of his career with Preston. He was a similar type to me. Whatever our faults, we'd run until we dropped and never knew when we were beaten. Later, I came across him when he was in charge of Huddersfield. I was looking after our reserve team and our goalkeeper, Tommy Younger, split his chin in a collision with their centre-forward. There was a right song and dance about it for a while, with director T.V. Williams, who later became Liverpool's first President, very upset. When Bill came in later, I said I thought it was a pure accident and things calmed down. That may have had a bearing later on the way we got on together at Liverpool.

In the August of 1959, I moved up to be first-team trainer after Albert Shelley retired. Bill came to take over as manager in December of that year. I never feared for the sack, although you know there's always a possibility when a new manager takes over.

Bill called us all together and made no bones about it - he was the boss. He said he would sort the team out. He would get you into conversation and you could sway him, but he was sorting it out. In the end, he stated there was a lot wrong at Liverpool, but the staff was all right, and he was keeping it.

There was no way you could not work for him. You get to know people and how they tick. I knew I could work with him and sometimes went out of my way to help. It was my job to do so. You can sense when people have a bit of respect for you, and we could feel that Bill had respect for us, and we for him and it paid off all along the line.

We were all working towards the same goal. We were in the Second Division and we all wanted to get into the First and get established. Under Bill, we went on to get there in a couple of years - and then went on to win things. He proved himself to be one of the greatest managers we've had in Britain.

What was he like to work with? Well, for a start it was never dull. As well as being one of the greatest managers, he was also one of the game's greatest characters. He had a marvellous sense of humour, and you certainly need that to survive in football. He loved a laugh and there was no way that his life at Liverpool was a misery. He liked to sleep well, eat well and loved to talk about football. If he couldn't talk about football, he would switch to boxing – another love of his.

When we were in Chicago he took five of us to Soldier's Field. He hunted the groundsman out and asked where Jack Dempsey had fought Gene Tunney in their famous heavyweight title fight. The groundsman pointed out the spot, so we played a three-a-side game over the area where the ring had been. He'd heard that Dempsey more or less lived on steaks – so Liverpool more or less lived on them, too. But even the prospect of meeting Jack Dempsey couldn't get Bill out the first night he arrived in America for our tour in 1964. He came out later than the rest of the party and when we met him in the lounge of our hotel in New York, I asked him if he wanted to visit Jack Dempsey's bar. He looked at his watch and said it was too late. I said it was only half past six, but he hadn't altered his watch since leaving England and said that as far as he was concerned it was half past eleven and no Yanks were going to tell him what time it was.

He didn't really like the States, even though he had this big thing about fighters like Dempsey and the gangsters of the prohibition days. The Americans didn't talk enough about football. He wore his blazer with the Liverpool badge on, and he couldn't understand why nobody recognised him!

There are so many stories about him it's now difficult to separate fact from fiction. But Bill was such a character, with such a quick wit, that you felt he could have done or said everything he was credited with.

Geoff Twentyman, Liverpool's chief scout, tells a story about playing under Bill at Carlisle. They had a rough first half, and were two goals down. Bill asked the captain, 'Why did you kick off that way?' The captain replied: 'Because I lost the toss.' 'What did you call?' asked Bill. 'Heads,' said the captain. 'Ah, you don't call heads,' was Bill's last word on the subject.

Only Bill could have got away with the things he got away with. We were playing a five-a-side one day with poles for goalposts. Bill said a shot had gone over the top and there was a bit of a dispute about it. But he didn't ask Ian St John or Ronnie Yeats, he asked Chris Lawler, the quiet man who hardly said a word about anything. Chris said it had gone in. Bill was furious: 'That's the first time you've spoken and you have to go and tell a lie.'

Another time, Chris was in the middle of his run of over three hundred consecutive appearances. Chris hurt his foot on the Saturday, and in training I told him to take it easy. Bill saw me talking to him and asked: 'What does that malingerer want now?'

Bill didn't like it when a player was injured. He didn't like to go into hospital to visit players when they were there, or go to see the handicapped. It wasn't that he disliked them, he just never relished it.

On a Friday morning, the day before a game, he detested it if you couldn't be definite about a player's fitness. I was the physiotherapist and I had to give a verdict before he would pick the team. He didn't like you to sit on the fence, he liked you to make a decision. He was an impatient man, but we never had a row about any of my decisions on fitness. In fact, in the fifteen years I worked with him we never had a row at all.

It's strange now to look back to Bill's arrival, knowing how he hated losing as much as anybody and more than most, and to recall his reaction to Liverpool's first game under his management. We were beaten 4–0 by Cardiff. We all looked for the reaction, but it was the sensible one. You wouldn't have known from it whether we'd won 4–0 or lost 4–0. He wasn't going to shout the odds that early.

We played the season through and finished third. We finished third the following season as well. In the present day, with three up and three down, that would have been enough to take us up to the First Division. But it might have been too early for us. Even when we were promoted as Second Division champions in 1962, we were still sorting it all out. We had got Yeats and St John, then Tommy Lawrence got into the team in goal – the famous building-through-the-middle principle. We all felt we were ready then. When you're preparing to go into the big time you have to be good enough to stay there. There's no way you are going to buy people who might get you there and then fold up.

That was Bill's policy and we agreed with it. His arrival was the making of Liverpool. Where the club would have finished up without him we'll never know. He was ready-made for Liverpool, and was quickly accepted for his enthusiasm. He might have been a more diplomatic man, but at that time it needed a character with his qualities. I'm quite sure Liverpool didn't know exactly what they got when they got Bill Shankly. I don't think anyone in his wildest dreams thought Bill could do what he eventually did for Liverpool.

I'm only too glad that I was around to help in those years, and to get to know that unique character. I knew every whim and fancy, all his likes and dislikes, what upset him and what pleased him. He's gone on record, as I have here, in stating that we never had an argument. I know that ninety-nine times out of a hundred I must have said the right thing to him when he was upset by something - whether it was the results, the board, the players or the Press. I think this was one way I did my work for him. I'm sure he would never underestimate what we did.

I know now from my years in the chair he left, that at certain times it's vitally important that there are no problems. Other members of the staff can stop these problems reaching you. I like to think I was able to stop problems from reaching Bill.

One of his greatest strengths was the power he had to motivate players. He got away with stuff in his tactical talks that I'm sure no other man could get away with. He did it all to build his players up. No other team had a forward line. Cruyff, Best, Charlton, Law - they couldn't play. I've seen Bill take the magnetised figures representing these players off the board and put them in his tracksuit pocket during a team talk. I've also heard him talk, as he did after our European Cup game against Ajax in 1966. He said that if this was European football they could keep it. It was too defensive. And they had beaten us 5-1!

He was a generous man, his bark being worse than his bite. This was something you got to know about him. Other people would take offence but often we would know what was coming before he said it. Then we'd all have a laugh together.

He was an impulsive man. We once drove all the way to Lincoln to watch a goalkeeper. It was a four-hour drive and we stopped at Doncaster to eat. We were late for the match, and we saw only about a quarter of an hour's play before Bill said; 'I've seen enough.' The goalkeeper had had nothing to do, but Bill had already decided he wasn't for us. I don't know what he saw, but he saw something.

He could be an infuriating man. I remember when we were down staying at Porthcawl before a match with Swansea. There were two old women in the television room of the hotel waiting to watch *Coronation Street*. There was boxing on the other channel, and Bill wanted to watch that. There were about fourteen of our players in the room too. Bill called for a vote – he thought he was being democratic. I walked out, I was too embarrassed to stay and watch.

I'm sure the story about him taking Nessie, his wife, to watch Accrington Stanley on her birthday is fictitious. There must have been times she didn't see anything of Bill at all, he was so wrapped up in his football.

When he was not involved, he was like a caged lion. That's why I say there was no way he could really be a part-time adviser. He had to be completely involved. This, I'm sure, caused him a great deal of frustration.

I remember a speech he made in which he talked about retirement. That word, he said, should be removed from the dictionary. When he went from Liverpool he said he'd had enough, but in the end, he found that the close involvement with football was the thing he missed most.

I tried to persuade him to stay, but he told me he wanted to make a complete break from the whole thing. The chairman tried to get him to change his mind. He was adamant. He went – and that's how I came into a job I didn't really want at the time, to hold the fort for a few months until a new man could take over. I stayed on to enjoy a number of triumphs, thanks to the help of a number of people. And through it all the enormous contribution of Bill during those fifteen wonderful years was never forgotten.

People showed what they thought of him when he died. The

church at West Derby was packed for his funeral and then weeks later the Anglican Cathedral in Liverpool was packed for a memorial service.

He was what football is all about. You never really get closely involved with the people you work with. But it was a privilege and an honour to have been allowed to work with him.

4 Rome

One ill-conceived and ill-timed announcement from the Football Association prevented Liverpool from completing a unique League, FA Cup and European treble in 1977.

Eight days before the Cup Final with Manchester United at Wembley, and before we had even clinched the First Division title, the FA announced that if a replay was needed it would be on 27 June – five weeks *after* Wembley and in the middle of Wimbledon fortnight!

I was utterly appalled when I heard the news and described it as outrageous and ridiculous. It was an indiscreet decision, and coming before the final it was an ill-timed announcement which could only have been made by someone who had never played the game.

It drastically altered our entire attitude to the game, because it made it a win-or-bust affair, and that in turn materially affected my team selection because it made me opt for a more adventurous three-man attack instead of the four-man midfield which I knew to be the best formation for us.

That announcement was the biggest psychological blow we could have suffered, and I saw the reaction of the players who had given everything for ten months to put themselves into a unique position. There was no way that those not involved in the Home Internationals and the summer tours could have gone out of training, and that would have meant them keeping at it all summer. And we were already scheduled to report back for the following season's training preparations on 12 July.

Yet it was typical of so many of the decisions of football administrators in this country. We had given the nation a team to be proud of, and the whole country was talking about a treble. Yet when any team is in with a chance of winning for our country international football prestige, obstacles are invariably put in their way rather than removed to make the task easier.

And going for a treble was very hard work indeed. In fact, it hadn't even crossed my mind until it was almost on top of us. After all, the League and Cup double had been achieved only four times, and two of those, by Aston Villa and Preston in the last century, hardly count because of the few games they had to play in those days.

In these days of European competition it has become even harder. In fact, I felt more pressure at the beginning of March when we were in the quarter-finals of the European Cup and the FA Cup and were neck-and-neck with Ipswich in the title race. In the space of one week the whole season could have fallen apart, because on the Wednesday we had to try to retrieve a 1–0 deficit in the home leg of the quarter-final with St Etienne, three days later faced Middlesbrough in the sixth round of the FA Cup, and the following Tuesday had a Mersey derby with Everton at Goodison Park.

Who could ever forget that night against the Frenchmen at Anfield? They had unluckily lost to Bayern Munich in the previous year's final and were generally regarded as one of the best teams in Europe, if not *the* best.

The atmosphere that night was electric. You could feel yourself tingling with it and I was reminded of a night twelve years earlier when we thrashed Inter-Milan 3–1 at Anfield. This time, however, it was a gripping match that had everyone on the edge of their seats. Kevin Keegan put us on the right road with a first-half goal, but just after half-time the Frenchmen got an equaliser from Bathenay. It was a sickener, because with away goals counting double, it meant we had to score twice more to go through.

Ray Kennedy grabbed a goal to give us hope, and then I sent on David Fairclough to replace John Toshack, who was injured, to try to vary the pattern – and Davie obliged with the overall winner just six minutes from the end.

Davie scored again in the 2–0 win over Middlesbrough and we

achieved a goalless draw at Everton to complete a hectic seven days. But no one thought that there would be even more hectic days to follow.

April was, perhaps, the key month. FC Zurich were beaten comfortably enough in the semi-finals of the European Cup, but we faced a more daunting task against our arch-rivals Everton in the semi-finals of the FA Cup. The game at Maine Road, Manchester, came just three days after we had become only the third English club to reach the European Cup Final.

And we were lucky to get another bite of the cherry against them. They had a late goal disallowed for a marginal off-side decision after playing much better than they had for weeks. When things break for you like that you tend to think that luck is on your side and that you'll win through in the end. Which is, of course, what happened in the replay four days later, although I have never been one to take things for granted.

In the League, we took nine points out of ten in April to open up a two-point lead at the top, and we had a game in hand. We were going to Wembley. We were going to Rome. And the League Championship was there for the taking. It was up to us and it was only then that the impossible seemed a faint possibility. We virtually clinched the title with a goalless draw at Coventry and made sure of it in another goalless draw against West Ham at Anfield on 14 May.

The atmosphere both during and after the match with West Ham was somehow unreal. I have never known a team to win the championship amid such relatively quiet and unemotional scenes. It was quite unlike the year before, when we had won it at Wolves and the fans were dancing and singing in the middle of a motorway during a traffic jam on the M6.

At Anfield that day it was as if they had taken a title triumph for granted, and I think the fans were already living in their minds the Cup Final with Manchester United which was due the following Saturday. And even in our dressing-room there was no champagne. Everybody sensed, without saying anything, that it was just the first round of a three-round contest.

I have always kept a match diary, in which I write a brief

summary of all the games we play. The morning after the West Ham game I wrote: 'The point won the championship for the second year in succession, but apart from that very important thing, the game had little to offer from a spectator's point of view.'

We still had a final League match away at Bristol City on the Monday, and while the result didn't matter it was still a tricky match. Coming just five days before the Cup Final it was a time when no player wanted to get injured yet, ironically, it is when players are trying to keep out of trouble that they are at their most vulnerable. Loss of concentration is what causes most injuries – not for the man who makes the mistake, but for the person put in trouble by a lackadaisical pass.

We already had John Toshack and Phil Thompson on the injured list, and Ian Callaghan was playing only his first game since being hurt against St Etienne. We couldn't afford any more knocks or we would have been right down to the bare boards. As it was, I left out Kevin Keegan, both to avoid aggravating a slight groin strain and to give him a break at a time when he was charging around everywhere with his commercial activities and his forthcoming transfer to Hamburg.

I also left out Joey Jones to avoid getting him into disciplinary trouble. He had already been booked several times and another would have put him in danger of suspension. Fortunately we escaped without any further injuries at Bristol and I recorded in my diary: 'There was little in the game from our point of view, having won the title the previous Saturday. Now and again we produced some good combinations but the whole game lacked bite.'

Clubs, by and large, don't like playing matches in Cup Final week, but in this case it might have been a good thing. Had we only been in with a chance of two competitions we would have had a break, but that in turn gives you more time to dwell on the matches ahead. But with our triple involvement in those hectic weeks in the spring of 1977 we just didn't have time to think ahead. Matches came so thick and fast that no sooner had one final whistle sounded than you were lining up for the next match. It got so hectic that at one stage I even forgot to put up the team-sheet!

The involvement with the League championship certainly took our minds off Wembley, and when we returned from Bristol we kept the routine as normal as possible. The players were given their normal post-match day off, but I didn't impose any curfews. At a time like that you expect players in their position to have self-control and, in any case, at Liverpool we always believed in treating our players like men.

On Wednesday and Thursday it was also business as usual, with training at Melwood in the mornings. But on Thursday afternoon we set off for an historic week when we boarded the train for London.

We stayed, as we often had before Wembley matches, at the Sopwell House, a quiet hotel surrounded by the Hertfordshire countryside just outside St Albans. Not that it's ever quiet at a Cup Finalist's hotel, with television crews pre-recording for the Saturday morning previews, the Press looking for last-minute features and photographs and the sales men and promotional men organising the players to boost anything from razor blades to chewing-gum.

On Friday morning we trained at Arsenal's training ground close by, and then at lunchtime I announced the team.

It was a moment I had been dreading because I knew that for two men it would mean disappointment, and for one in particular it would mean heartbreak. Memories of the moment in 1950, when I learned I was left out of the Liverpool Cup Final side after scoring a goal in the semi-final, flooded back to me. My heart went out to Ian Callaghan, one of the greatest servants the club had ever had, when I named him only substitute, and I could have cried for David Fairclough, the hero against St Etienne, when I had to tell him that he would not even be getting stripped.

I had made the decision a couple of days earlier, but there was nothing to be gained by announcing it then. The days of announcing your Cup Final side at the beginning of the week are long since past. You have to try to keep your entire squad on their toes as long as possible and if one is left out he loses his self-discipline and starts to take it easy. You find that players in a similar boat tend to pair off together and lead each other into trouble. And you can't afford that, in case you have a last-minute training injury or accident and have to call on one of those players whose attitude is all wrong.

That FA decision had swayed me into playing David Johnson up front with Kevin Keegan and Steve Heighway, because I couldn't bear the thought of a replay. And later I regretted not playing Ian Callaghan as a fourth man in midfield, because I'm sure we would not have lost if I had used what I knew to be our most effective formation.

The media had a slight influence too. All the calls for a final to remember and open attacking football helped force me to surrender and play three front men when I knew that the other system invariably gave us more attacking options. That was to be proved in Rome.

I tried to ensure that all the ballyhoo was finished by the time the players went to bed on the Friday night. They get roused by it, and at that stage they ought to be calming down. If it went on into Saturday morning, then by kick-off time they would be mentally drained. Our policy was always to play down matches like Cup Finals as much as possible because Wembley, even to people like us who had been there so often, is an unnerving experience.

Almost inevitably the players were up earlier on Cup Final morning than on normal Saturdays. They were supposed to be resting, but with television having played the game in advance on the Friday night, there was no way their minds could be at rest. I tried to calm them down by being as natural as possible, but players react to nerves in different ways.

You would not have thought Ray Kennedy, for example, had any nerves, as he appeared so relaxed on these big occasions. Because of this people called him casual - but that was not the case. Ray Clemence went very quiet, whereas usually he was one of the noisy ones. While Terry McDermott was another who liked to charge around. He'd got to be active and the nerves showed when he started clowning about.

But it all blended together although by and large the tenser the occasion the quieter the dressing-room. The theme of my pre-match talk was about us rather than Manchester United, because I was more concerned with how we played, knowing that at our best we could beat anybody. As we were playing three front runners, I had to make slight adjustments and I also mentioned set pieces, both ours and United's, but I didn't labour the points because it was more important for us to impose our pattern on the game.

In the tunnel, as we were waiting to go into the stadium, I shook hands with Tommy Docherty and said I hoped it would be a good game. I wasn't going to be hypocritical and wish him good luck!

Leading out a team at Wembley is the most pleasing and proud thing you can do, for it is an acknowledgement of what you have achieved in the season. It is one of the highlights of your career and many managers would give their right arm for the chance. As you walk out, your mind is in turmoil. You're playing the game yourself, anticipating moves and destroying them. My wife and family were there, but I didn't wave to them. It was no disrespect to them because my mind was elsewhere.

The following season when we played Nottingham Forest in the League Cup Final, the same sort of thing must have happened to Brian Clough, because he went marching off on his own and had almost overtaken the official who was leading us out, before he realised what he was doing, and came back and apologised.

Even at that late stage, the players are still in your charge and you have to try to act as normally as possible to prevent them detecting that you are nervous. But it's a marvellous moment. Losing in the semi-finals of the Cup is the worst time because you are so near, yet so far. Losing at Wembley is different, because at least you have been there, and less than two hours later when we had lost 2–1, I could still feel pride.

We played well and lost to two goals that had an element of luck about them. At half-time, with the score at 0–0, I knew we had been the better side but had not taken our chances. There wasn't much I could say to the team, apart from reminding them to concentrate more when chances arose.

Ray Clemence should have saved Stuart Pearson's shot for the opening goal, even though it was well placed and not easy to deal with. It was the sort of shot you usually use your foot to stop, but what can you say to a great goalkeeper? Even the greatest people in the world make mistakes, and you can't criticise someone for a moment of human error, least of all at Wembley.

When Jimmy Case equalised so quickly I thought we would go on to win. It was the best goal of the game, because United's winner was a pure fluke. Lou Macari's shot was going yards wide until it hit Jimmy Greenhoff and deflected into the net. But even though we lost we performed with credit and had nothing to be ashamed of. In fact our performance was as good as any we gave in those three crucial matches.

There was no great disappointment that the great dream of the treble had ended, because at least we were League champions, and there was no way I was going to Rome feeling disappointed. Although Jock Stein and Sir Matt Busby had led British teams into European Cup finals before, I was only the second Englishman to do so after Jimmy Armfield with Leeds in 1975. I was looking forward to it.

We travelled straight home from Wembley because, with our trip to Rome the next week, we decided against staying another night in London for a banquet and then travelling home for a tour of the city. It was the European Cup Final, and it was the preparations for that which were important then – not celebrations when a job was only half done.

Naturally the players were depressed as they began the journey home, and it was up to me to try to get them back into the right frame of mind. It was then, on the train home, that fate stepped in to guide our hands. One of the special trains ahead of us broke down and we were stuck for almost two hours. Of course there was alcohol on the train, and the players were drinking – not to excess, but to help drown the disappointment. In that state of mind you don't need much, and that extra couple of hours or so in the train was all they needed to switch from depression to defiance. By the time we drew into Lime Street Station they were ready to take on Borussia Moenchengladbach there and then.

Top professional footballers are like thoroughbred racehorses, they are highly strung and very susceptible to atmosphere. If their heads had stayed down, there was no way they would have won in Rome, and if that train had been on time they would probably have gone home in the wrong frame of mind. Those extra drinks got it out of their system, and nobody stepped out of line. There might have been one or two clowns in the team, but we treated them like men and expected them to behave likewise.

The people who sit in the stand perhaps don't realise the extra pressure exerted by the emotional side of the game. It is not easy to cope with, and it is quite possible to become drunk on four ounces of wine gums! But I knew as I left the party at Lime Street and headed for home that the players' attitude was all right. They knew they still had a job to do.

I had a quick drink when I got home to help me relax and went to bed. The post-match reaction is probably worse after a Cup Final than at any other time, because you are constantly replaying the game in your mind. But I had begun to make plans for the game in Rome and I had already reached a conclusion about the formation I would play. I picked the team then, on Saturday night. The final stage of the incredible journey through that season had begun.

It was business as usual on Sunday. I went to Anfield as I always did, in case players reported in with injuries, but fortunately there were none. I reached for my diary and wrote: 'The only disappointing thing about Wembley was the result, because we dominated the first half and should have been ahead at the interval. Manchester United opened the scoring and Jimmy Case scored a brilliant equaliser, only for us to lose to an unlucky goal. Now we must get the team into the right frame of mind for the most important game in Liverpool's history.'

The players reported in for training on the Monday and went through the normal routine prior to a midweek match. They didn't seem to be suffering any adverse reaction from the defeat at Wembley and they were reasonably relaxed. We trained again on Tuesday morning and then it was time for the off and our charter flight to Leonardo da Vinci Airport, Rome. The Eternal City. A perfect setting.

We settled into the Holiday Inn and a local semi-professional club loaned us their all-weather pitch to train on the following morning. Not that we did much, in Rome's heat, apart from just loosen up. The sense of occasion, the weather, and the culmination of ten months of football dictated that the players should keep as much strength as possible for the game itself.

We knew all about Moenchengladbach because we had played them in the final of the UEFA Cup four years earlier, and they were a typical German side, skilful and disciplined.

I had seen their semi-final with Dynamo Kiev on television as we rested before our semi-final in Zurich, and Tom Saunders had watched them five or six times. We knew about the threat from Allan Simonsen with his lethal finishing, but there were a couple of things going for us. Jupp Heynckes, who had put us on the rack and scored twice in the second leg of that 1973 final, had a knee problem, and their elder statesman Herbert Wimmer was getting on. Indeed, he cracked up in the game with a muscle injury.

I also knew about their fear of John Toshack's height. Even though he had not played since he was injured against St Etienne, I kept him in the squad. I knew he would not play because I knew in my mind that he wasn't fit, but I'd almost convinced John that he'd be in the side.

I wanted to keep the Germans thinking that way, so that they would adapt their tactics to counter the threat of his height. The Germans are so disciplined that even when they find out they have made a mistake in their planning, their thinking is too rigid to allow them to change.

Tosh frightened them to death and had played a significant part in building up the 3-0 lead in the home leg which was the foundation of our triumph against Borussia in 1973. The original game was abandoned because of a freak rain storm, and John wasn't playing. But enough had been learned in the twenty-five minutes or so that were played for us to realise that it was essential for him to play the following night when the game was replayed.

And to fox the Germans further, and convince them I was

planning to cash in on their fear of height, I also included Alan Waddle in the squad. It was not until the morning of the match that I told the players that neither of them would be playing.

Udo Lattek, their manager, had watched us in the semi-finals and, although Tosh hadn't played he was convinced I was keeping him under wraps especially for Borussia. How much that kidology helped I don't know, but I had known since Saturday night what my team would be.

I named the team which finished at Wembley, with Ian Callaghan taking his normal place in midfield and David Johnson on the substitutes' bench, leaving the front-running to Kevin Keegan and Steve Heighway. It was the team I should have played against Manchester United, and if I had I'm convinced we wouldn't have lost.

On the other hand, if Cally had played at Wembley it's doubtful whether he would have been as fresh as he was in Rome. What is more, if we had achieved the League and Cup double, would we have been so determined to win the greatest prize of all?

As it was, I have never seen a team so relaxed before a match. It was as if a great weight had been lifted from everyone's shoulders and that they realised they just had to make one last effort; that they had to go out there and do their best - and if that wasn't good enough, well, so be it.

Yet it was like that famous showbiz phrase - it'll be all right on the night. After all the pressure of the previous two months, the effort to make sure the players' attitude was right and the preparations thorough, this was the end. As the players were led out on to the field there was nothing more I could do. The ball was at their feet. That giant urn, the European Cup, perched high up in the Olympic Stadium, was up for grabs.

The whole thing, however, was perfect, from the setting and the relative cool of the evening to the impeccable behaviour of the supporters, who were truly magnificent and played a real part in Liverpool's finest hour.

We were soon well on top and we scored a goal which I can only describe as a coaching showpiece. Kevin Keegan, who was giving that great professional Berti Vogts a dog's life, had the

German selling programmes to the crowd – so far had he pulled him away from where the build-up was taking place. He was the key defender, and he didn't realise what was happening until it was too late. Borussia were spreadeagled as Ian Callaghan won the ball in midfield and pushed it out to Steve Heighway on the right. Cally followed on down the flank, pulling the Germans even wider and allowing Steve to cut inside and play the ball into Terry McDermott's path. It was a perfect example of Terry's awareness, anticipation and running at their best, and he scored magnificently.

At half-time I warned them against feeling complacent because they were so comfortably in control, but afterwards Jimmy Case made a mistake with a back pass to Phil Neal and Simonsen was on to it in a flash and demonstrated his lethal finishing with a tremendous shot.

We were back to square one and the game was wide open. It was then that the Germans got a break, and Ray Clemence produced one of his most memorable saves from Uli Stielike. He might have made more spectacular saves, but I doubt he has made many more important ones, because that was the turning-point of the game and the Germans never recovered from it.

Only a few minutes later we were back in the lead thanks to Tommy Smith. I can't remember him ever scoring with his head before, but it was one that even Dixie Dean would have been proud of, and stemmed again from Borussia's fear of high crosses. Larry Lloyd had scored a similar goal in that 1973 final. The Germans were so disciplined that they followed the big men like Ray Kennedy, who were acting as decoys at a corner, and they were dragged away from the danger area. They were vulnerable to a man arriving late into a space – and that's exactly what Tommy Smith did as Steve Heighway's corner came over, and it was a perfect header.

It was yet another perfect part of a perfect night, for a goal in a European Cup Final – and the vital goal at that – was a fitting climax to a magnificent career. Liverpool had never won anything without Tommy Smith, because he was one of those personalities, very few and far between, who can cope with tension and actually improve as the tension increases.

He had illustrated that in the semi-final in Zurich, where he had given away a penalty from which they took the lead, and then been booked – all in the first quarter of an hour. Yet a few minutes later he was left in a one-against-one situation in the penalty area where if a goal was to be prevented a perfect tackle was needed. It also needed courage, for the consequences for Tommy of a mistake were not only another penalty but probably a sending-off. Yet he came away with the ball after a tackle which was a model of timing and execution.

Tommy's goal was the final nail in Borussia's coffin, for there was no way they were going to come back from that, but just to make sure Phil Neal scored from the penalty spot after the out-thought, out-played, out-manoevred, frustrated and dejected Berti Vogts finally committed one foul too many on Kevin Keegan – and this time in the penalty area.

Phil Neal is by and large a cool customer, and even such a big occasion didn't over-awe him. He beat Kneibs deliberately and precisely, but in later years the mass exposure of his technique eventually caught up with him as goalkeepers began to read him.

Yet despite Liverpool's 3–1 victory, which owed so much to a great team effort, one man stood out in particular, for he used that final in Rome to play his finest game for Liverpool in his last match for the club – Kevin Keegan. By then he was more or less transferred to Hamburg, but his performance in Rome proved that he was worth every Mark the Germans paid for him.

Kevin had a wanderlust, and he played really well in about only half a dozen games for Liverpool that season, because of his frustration and desire to move on. In turn, the crowd became frustrated with him, which was understandable because they knew he was a good player and they didn't want to lose him. And I'm sure if he had turned in a performance against Manchester United like the one he gave against the Germans we would have won the FA Cup. The question is, however, could he have run like that twice in so few days? Nevertheless his was an excellent performance with which to crown his career with Liverpool.

Winning the European Cup in Rome was the greatest moment of my life, and it was appropriate that history should be made in an historic city. I was the first English manager to win the European Cup and I couldn't have picked a better time or place to do it. Everything was perfect. Even now I can feel the emotion welling up inside me whenever I watch a film, centred around that European Cup Final in Rome, called *Hope in their Hearts*.

Memories flooded back, too, as the team coach left the stadium and threaded its way through those ancient streets back to the hotel. I had driven into Rome in 1944 in a 15 cwt truck with the Anti-Tank Regiment, but if anyone had told me then that thirty-three years later I'd be back to win the European Cup I'd probably have been shot because I would have gone out celebrating.

Yet I refused to have a drink during the riotous all-night party which followed our triumph. As with most people, I like a drink and enjoy celebrating a great victory - but this was different. This was no ordinary celebration because this was no ordinary triumph. To qualify for the European Cup, you have to win the First Division Championship - which I have always regarded as the true test of a team - and then, to win it, you have to beat the best teams in Europe. There is nothing ordinary about that.

We had won the League and the European Cup, and had come so close to winning the FA Cup as well, that it is foolish for people to say the treble will never be won. We damned nearly proved it could.

But that night back at the Holiday Inn, at St Peter's in Rome, with a buffet magnificent enough to have fed my regiment throughout the war, and with enough champagne to have sunk Noah's Ark, I wanted to remain sober. I was drinking it all in - the atmosphere, the sense of pride, of achievement, of joy and reward for ten months' hard labour.

It was a unique and very special occasion and I wanted to savour every moment of it. I wasn't going to miss out on any of it by getting drunk. In fact, probably the only sober men in Rome that night were me, the Pope and Horace Yates, the teetotal Sports Editor of the *Liverpool Daily Post*.

I knew I could let my hair down later in Spain when the players and coaching staff went on holiday. You can find an excuse to get drunk at any time, but you can't recreate an occasion like that night in Rome.

My match diary read as follows: 'After Saturday's defeat at Wembley we wondered what effect it would have on the players. We need not have worried, because right from the start we dominated the game and turned in the best performance in the history of the club.'

5 European Odyssey

In the heady glory of Rome, who would have believed we would stay in the European Cup for so many consecutive seasons, and march onwards to establish Liverpool as the most successful British team ever in Continental competition? And who would have believed what lay ahead of us when, back in September 1976, we needed a penalty by Phil Neal to add to a goal by John Toshack to give us a 2–0 lead over Crusaders, the Belfast part-timers?

It was an inconspicuous start to what was to be a glorious season, and I remember the Ulstermen packing their penalty area at Anfield and making it extremely difficult for us to find the space to create chances. One of their players lost a contact lens during the game and I told him, 'There's only one place it will be – in the penalty area!'

We had a nasty experience of another kind when we went to Belfast for the return leg. Because of the troubles in the province, UEFA gave us special dispensation and allowed us to travel on the day of the match instead of the day before as their rules state. We planned to have a light work-out at Melwood, fly out in mid-morning, have lunch and then go to their Seaview ground for the match, before returning home straight afterwards. But the best laid plans of mice and men....

When we got to Speke Airport there was no plane! It was fogbound in Leeds, so we had to travel back into Liverpool for lunch at an hotel. It was 1.30 before the plane finally arrived and we were able to make the trip, and as it was an afternoon kick-off the players had to change in the bus on the way to the ground. There were more surprises and shocks in store for us at Seaview. Nobody could complain about the hospitality offered by

Crusaders, for one of their officials came into our dressing-room before the game and offered the players a drink of whisky!

Naturally it was refused, but perhaps they could have done with it to brace themselves for some early shocks on the field, because Crusaders hurled themselves at us from the kick-off and had a couple of chances as well as hitting the woodwork. We weathered the storm, however, and David Johnson scored a couple of goals, with Kevin Keegan, Steve Heighway and Terry McDermott, who had come on as substitute, also getting on the scoresheet to give us a 5–0 win and a comfortable passage into the next round with a 7–0 aggregate.

It was then that we had to get the atlas out, for we were drawn against a team few people in this country had ever heard of – Trabzonspor. We finally located it in the far north-east of Turkey on the Black Sea coast, barely one hundred miles from the borders with Russia and Iran. We knew right away that it was going to be anything but an easy ride, but even a pessimist would not have envisaged the problems and conditions which lay ahead. They began when Aer Lingus, who flew us to most of our European matches, found that the runway at Trabzon Airport was too short to accommodate the aircraft they would have to operate for such a long flight. As there was also a big time difference to overcome, we amended our normal European schedule and flew out for the first leg on the Monday instead of the day before the match. We stayed that night in Ankara, and the following day took an internal Turkish Airlines flight for the final 500-mile flight into the unknown.

As we dipped sharply towards the Black Sea, after crossing the 14,000-foot Anatolian Mountains which dropped steeply into the sea, we saw Aer Lingus's point – the single runway began on the edge of a cliff and ended with a brick wall, beyond which was a road and the mountains. There were some butterflies in a few stomachs in the cabin as we made our approach, I can tell you.

The Turkish way of organising their soccer is a lot different from our own, as we found out as soon as we had passed through the airport formalities and were boarding the coach. The Press has a loud say in what happens in their football, and the journalists who were travelling with us were approached and asked if they minded the kick-off time being brought forward. We were not consulted by the Turks at first, but the British Press lads pointed them in our direction. Apparently Miss Turkey was due to kick the match off and the Turks wanted to put pictures of the ceremony on a flight to Istanbul which took off at the scheduled kick-off time.

It was not our only experience of the power of the Press in Turkey, for when we arrived at the stadium there were tables and chairs for the journalists - but no accommodation for our directors and officials!

That was just about the last straw after a nightmare first glimpse at Trabzon. It's an industrial port which straggles along the thin coastal strip, with the main square at the top of a steep hill rising up the mountains. The bus stopped in the square outside an hotel, which was not the one we had been told we were staying in, but one which the Turks insisted was the best in town. That said it all about that town!

I told everyone to stay on the bus while I went to make an inspection, and I was horrified by what I saw. It was a doss-house, and if you said it had a star rating it was only because you could see them through the holes in the roof. But we were stuck with it and just had to make the best of a bad job. It was a squalid place, with food to match and the sanitation leaving a lot to be desired. The players existed just on chocolate they had brought from England and it was a wise move because some other members of the party contracted a rather vicious stomach bug, while others complained of bed bugs. It was a thoroughly nasty experience, and we had to stop there for two nights!

Even the Press, who were given the red carpet treatment by their Turkish counterparts, had their share of problems with communications. Phone calls were delayed for up to seven hours and one journalist sat for ten hours trying to get an international telex line.

It just made us all the more determined to beat the Turks where it mattered - out on the pitch. But even then we were thwarted.

The little oval stadium was not exactly the most luxurious I'd ever been to and it had a strange setting. It resembled Rorke's Drift, with the mountains towering above and thousands of people sitting on the hillside with a 'grandstand' or rather bird's eye view of the match. The pitch was as rough as everything else, but we thought we had the situation in hand until Trabzon were awarded a dubious penalty in the second half for an alleged foul by Emlyn Hughes. Cemil scored from the spot and we were beaten 1–0.

We weren't too concerned, however, because the Turks hadn't shown anything to be alarmed about, and we were confident we could turn the tables in the return leg at Anfield. We were just glad to take off from Trabzon and head for home.

Indeed the second game provided few problems as David Johnson, Kevin Keegan and Steve Heighway gave us a 3–0 win and a 3–1 aggregate triumph. The only disappointment was the attitude of the Turks in defeat. When they realised they were on their way out of the competition they kicked up rough.

But we were through, and then it was the relative ease and comfort of St Etienne and the thoroughly western and sedate atmosphere of Zurich en route to the glory of Rome.

Trabzon, however, with its Eastern atmosphere, yashmaks and wailing Muslims and no Turkish delight, had a unique place in our recent history, for that game was the only one which Phil Neal missed since becoming a regular member of the side in 1974. Lucky Phil. If there was one trip to miss it was that one.

That bizarre season, ending as it did in such a triumphant way, more than compensated for our earlier disappointments in the European Cup – the biggest of which was our defeat by Inter-Milan in the semi-finals in 1965. That season had been our first experience of European competition, and after beating Reykjavik (11–1), Anderlecht (4–0) and Cologne, on the spin of a disc after a 2–2 draw in a play-off in Rotterdam, we were confident we could go all the way. We were even more convinced of it when, on one of the most emotional nights in Anfield history after the FA Cup had been paraded before the crowd for the first time, we hammered Inter-Milan 3–1. It should have been 4–1, for Chris Lawler had a perfectly good goal disallowed, and it was so painful for the

Inter coach Helenio Herrera to watch his team being comprehensively beaten that he turned and sat the other way in the dug-out, facing the wall.

We have always maintained that we were robbed of the European Cup that year, for when we went to the San Siro for the return there was no way we were going to qualify for the final with Benfica. The referee was a Spaniard whose name I shall never forget - Ortiz de Mendibil. He allowed two goals which we felt were blatantly illegal. The ball was literally kicked out of Tommy Lawrence's hands for one of them and it surely was no coincidence that we never heard of him again. This experience alerted us to the tricks that Continental teams get up to in an effort to unsettle and unnerve you.

Two years later we were champions again and back in the European Cup. We also had our first taste of playing an Iron Curtain team, Petrolul Ploesti, from the oil-producing area of Rumania. A 2-0 win at Anfield and a 1-3 defeat over there forced another play-off, this time in Brussels, which we won 2-0. Then it was on to Amsterdam - and an encounter with Ajax and a certain Johan Cruyff, then a teenager and barely heard of. On a foggy night in the Olympic Stadium he destroyed us. We lost 5-1, and Cruyff turned on the magic again at Anfield where we were held to a 2-2 draw and said goodbye to the European Cup for seven years.

It is a strange fact that throughout all Liverpool's years in Europe the second round was always our vulnerable stage. Invariably the first round produced a relatively easy game against weak opposition, and by the time the quarter-finals and later stages arrived in March, we were hitting peak form and challenging for the title. But the second round in October was invariably a stumbling block, and it certainly was in 1973 when we returned to the European Cup after winning a League and UEFA Cup double.

That time it was the Yugoslavs, Red Star Belgrade, who beat us. We made hard work of beating the no-hopers of Jeunesse d'Esch of Luxemburg in the first round, drawing 1-1 away and winning only 2-0 at home, but then came up against the much stronger Red Star. They became only the second foreign team to win at Anfield – Ferencvaros of Hungary were the first – when with a display of powerful, accurate shooting they won 2–1 and completed our exit with a similar scoreline in Belgrade.

All those disappointments were forgotten that May night in Rome in 1977, but the following season it was back to business. As I've always said, you get nothing for what you achieved yesterday, so when we lined up at Anfield against our old rivals Dynamo Dresden, whom we had beaten twice in the past in victorious UEFA Cup campaigns, we had to forget Rome. The players responded magnificently and showed we meant to take the defence of the European Cup very seriously indeed. The goals were scored by Jimmy Case (2), Ray Kennedy, Alan Hansen and Phil Neal (penalty) as we beat Dynamo 5–1.

The morning after that demolition of Dynamo I wrote in my diary: 'This was a very good win and the victory made them look much worse than they are. We took our chances well and we got the goals at the right time. It should stand us in good stead for the return, which should be a good game, but we can take nothing for granted.'

My suspicions about Dresden proved well founded, for we had anything but an easy ride in the return and were very thankful for that four-goal lead. I wrote afterwards: 'My impression that Dynamo Dresden are a better team than they were made to look at Anfield was more than confirmed. They played brilliantly, and only our 5–1 lead kept them at bay. I don't think I've seen a team play as fast as they did and for so long. I'd tried to have a quiet game, but they harried us over every yard of the pitch and it was not until I introduced David Fairclough to run at them that we got into the game a bit.'

The move worked, for we managed to score through Steve Heighway at a time when Dresden were 2–0 up on the day and threatening to push us all the way. That goal knocked the stuffing out of them, for then they needed three more goals even to force extra time. We held on, and although we lost the match 2–1 we went through on a 6–3 aggregate to qualify for a quarter-final tie against those famous Eagles of Lisbon, Benfica, on 1 March.

We had been given a bye in the first round because there were only thirty-one entrants in the competition, the Albanians having been ruled out by disciplinary sanctions. So there we were, only four games away from a second consecutive appearance in the final.

Rarely, however, can the Estadio da Luz – the Stadium of Light – have been so dark. March came in like a lion in Lisbon that year, for I don't think I can remember conditions like it. The rain was torrential, resembling a tropical storm, and all the way round the huge, crater-like stadium the fans were huddled under umbrellas. It was as if 80,000 black beetles were watching the match – it was a weird sight.

But we produced a magnificent performance, and goals from Jimmy Case and Emlyn Hughes gave us a 2–1 win in the first leg which was far more than we had dared dream of. Afterwards I wrote: 'The game was played in some of the worst conditions I have seen in my career. On a very heavy pitch it poured down continuously throughout the game and perhaps it was a little fortunate that it was possible to finish. It was, however, a tremendous result for us and should put us in good heart for the return.'

Indeed it did, for we got off to a great start with two quick goals to make the overall result a formality. Ian Callaghan, Kenny Dalglish, Terry McDermott and Phil Neal scored our goals as we won 4–1 on the night and 6–2 on aggregate, and my comments were: 'Two early goals just about put paid to Benfica's chances. We played well in that early period, but later individuals took over and we lost a bit of our rhythm. Benfica got a goal back from a Jimmy Case back pass but I suppose they were still disappointed. But it was the same old story – they can only play as well as you let them.'

Our next stop was West Germany and our great rivals Borussia Moenchengladbach in the semi-finals. We had beaten them not only in Rome the year before but also in the final of the UEFA Cup in 1973, so we knew we had a psychological advantage. We also had the knowledge that Borussia Dortmund, in the final of the 1966 European Cup Winners' Cup, and Bayern Munich, in the same competition in 1972, had been the only German teams to beat us in goodness knows how many matches against teams from that country. And, just as we preferred it, we were away in the first leg.

In fact, we lost 2–1 in the horse-shoe shaped Rhine Stadium in Düsseldorf in the first leg, but we had scored an away goal, by David Johnson, which can often be crucial, and felt aggrieved that we had not drawn. Rainer Bonhof, that dead-ball expert, had given Borussia their single goal advantage in the closing minutes with a vicious, swerving, dipping free-kick, which also took a deflection – and it should never have been a free kick in the first place.

My after-match notes read: 'We were unfortunate to concede a goal from a free kick from Bonhof in the last minutes. Borussia probably had the better of the first half, but we never lost our composure and had the better chances. Two unfortunate decisions cost us the goals. The first goal from Hannes came from a corner which should have been a goal-kick, and Phil Thompson was pushed on to the ball for the handling offence which produced the free kick from which they scored their second. But the tie is still wide open and it is up to us to force the pace in the return.'

There were more than 51,000 at Anfield for the return. The atmosphere was just right because we needed an early goal, and Ray Kennedy duly provided it after only seven minutes. At that point we were at Wembley for the final but we daren't relax in case Borussia snatched an away goal to cancel out the one we had scored in the Rhine Stadium. I need not have worried, however, for we went on to win 3–0 on the night for a convincing 4–2 aggregate victory to earn a clash with Belgian champions, Bruges, to defend our European crown in the final at Wembley.

Only four days before beating Borussia we had struggled to beat Leicester, who were subsequently relegated, 3–2 at Anfield in the First Division. But we put those problems behind us against the Germans, and I recalled: 'It was a splendid performance because, as we were trailing 2–1, we needed an early goal. We got it in the seventh minute and then took complete control. It was a real team effort which made the Leicester game on the Saturday look a farce. Still, history has been made because we are the first English club to reach the final in consecutive years.'

10 May 1978 was notable because we retained the European Cup by beating Bruges at Wembley in the final, but it will never be remembered as a thrilling football occasion. That was not our fault, however, because while we wanted to go out to try to entertain the crowd, the Belgians seemed intent purely on survival, with the chance, perhaps, of stealing the cup on a penalty shoot-out after extra time.

They had the excuse that a couple of key men were missing because of injury but, for me, even that could not excuse their blatantly negative attitude. I wrote: 'It was far and away a poorer game than last year and when we played them in the UEFA Cup Final in 1976. Bruges were depleted by injuries but they never tried to play and were quite content to keep the score respectable. In no way was it a classic but we dominated from start to finish and were worthy winners.'

In fact it needed that spark of individualism to give us victory and it came from two Scots who were both comparatively new to our set-up – Graeme Souness and Kenny Dalglish.

Graeme had joined us only four months earlier from Middlesbrough and had been eligible only for the semi-finals and final. But it was his sense of awareness and his vision which allowed him to spot the opening and provide Kenny with the sort of opportunity on which he thrives. Kenny was given a one-to-one situation with the goalkeeper in which he had time to think and he waited for Jensen to commit himself before calmly chipping the ball over him into the net. I sensed then that one goal would be enough because of the Belgians' attitude, but my heart was in my mouth later on when Alan Hansen, another newcomer, made a mistake which could so easily have led to an equaliser and extra time.

Nevertheless we joined the élite band of clubs to have won the cup not only on two occasions but in two consecutive years, and it was our ambition even then, in the Wembley dressing-room after the match, to go on to join Real Madrid, Ajax and Bayern Munich as the only teams to have won it three times on the trot.

But even before we left Wembley for our celebrations in London I warned that our biggest stumbling block could be Nottingham Forest who had been guided by Brian Clough to the League

The Bishop Auckland team that won the FA Amateur Cup in 1939.

Breakfast in El Alamein, 13 July 1942, with my old mates Jim Bates, Jack Bennett and Joe Beal.

Before embarkation – kitted out for Egypt with my mate Frank Owen.

Rest time in Cairo, 1941.

The Army team in Italy. Thirty-three years later I go back to Rome to win the European Cup.

Meeting Gus Lesnevich on the *Queen Mary* in 1946. He was over here to fight the late Freddie Mills.

Off to Holland with the England 'B' team. Can you spot Ron Greenwood, the former England manager?

Bob Paisley, Liverpool FC.

The Liverpool line-up in the 1948/49 season.

The team with manager Don Welsh in 1951.

A break at Blackpool with some of the 1960s team.

Giving the amateurs a hand. With Colin Bridge of Skelmersdale before their first visit to Wembley in the FA Amateur Cup in 1967.

Winners of the FA Cup and the Charity Shield, 1965.

Back from Bruges. The grins are because the trophy fell in half and Emlyn and I were holding it together.

Sizing up the opposition – Tom Saunders and I watch Zürich before meeting them in the 1977 European Cup.

Success is sweet – I share a toast with captain Emlyn Hughes and chairman John Smith.

championship in their first season back in the First Division.

Whether UEFA or the rest of Europe wanted two English teams in the European Cup the following season I wouldn't know, but the odds against us drawing Forest in the first round were long, even though we were seeded and they weren't. But that's how the draw went, and I can still feel the utter dejection I suffered when we were beaten by them.

We lost the first leg at Nottingham 2–0, partly because when playing against a team from your own country the players tend to treat it as a League match. When we were a goal down we were looking for an equaliser instead of accepting that as a reasonable result in the first leg of a European Cup tie. The outcome of that adventure was a second Forest goal which gave us a mountain to climb in the return at Anfield.

'It was very disappointing,' I recorded. 'Forest harrassed us out of our game and we had players who would not compete. They marked our midfield tightly, and when Forest were in possession they asked for no build-up from their midfield, but, instead by-passed them with long balls up the middle. We had difficulty mastering their front men and now we have a real fight on our hands.'

Garry Birtles and Colin Barrett had scored the goals at Nottingham, and we all knew it would take something special if we were to reverse the scoreline. It was not to be, even though we dominated a goal-less game and, very depressed in my office the next morning, I wrote: 'Once again we were unable to score against a side which we completely outplayed from start to finish. The first half was as well as we'd played, but in the frenzied atmosphere we hurried our best chances and were very disappointed to go out in the first round of a competition which I honestly believed we could win for a third time.'

As soon as I'd closed my diary I picked up the telephone and rang my bookie to place a bet on Forest to win the European Cup – that's how confident I had been that we would win it. So I was doubly delighted when they beat Malmo to win the trophy, both as an Englishman and as a punter!

Having regained the League championship, we were back in

the European Cup the following season – as, of course, were Forest as holders. Surely, I thought to myself, they cannot pair us together again. You hope, and half expect, to get a soft touch in the first round against a team from, say, Luxemburg, Cyprus, Malta, Iceland or such like, without meaning any disrespect to those nations. But even with a seeding system you get some very good teams who are not seeded, such as Forest the year before.

Our luck was out again as we drew the powerful Russians of Dynamo Tbilisi. The first leg was at Anfield, but we were without Ray Kennedy. This was a considerable blow because, as he had demonstrated in the past and was to do again in the future, he could score goals when the pressure was on. Alan Hansen was also missing, so I drafted in Colin Irwin and David Fairclough and moved Jimmy Case to the left-half berth.

It didn't take long to realise that we had a real fight on our hands, because in players like Kipiani, Chevadje, Shengalia and Gutsaev, the Russians – or strictly speaking the Georgians – had real skill. My post-match diary read: 'This was a tremendous battle against a very confident and skilful side. Now only a tremendous performance will get us a result over there. Our three men in midfield never got to grips with their opponents and although we dominated the second half we could not get a decisive lead in the tie.'

We had to settle for a 2–1 lead, thanks to goals from David Johnson and Jimmy Case, to take with us behind the Iron Curtain. But our problems did not end there, and anyone in this country who thinks Communism is the answer to our political problems would quickly have thought again if he had experienced the trip we had to make.

For a start we were not allowed to charter from the airline of our choice. The Russian authorities insisted that they would allow in only a national carrier, British Airways, and then only as far as Moscow. The rest of the journey would have to be with their own airline, Aeroflot. Nor were we allowed to fly direct to Tbilisi, the capital of Soviet Georgia in the deep south of the country between the Black and Caspian Seas.

To try to reduce the problems we chartered Aeroflot for the

full flight from Speke to Tbilisi and back, but still the Russians insisted on the dog-leg flight via Moscow, where we had to put down for seemingly interminable immigration procedures, while they searched the hand luggage, which we had to leave on the plane - presumably for 'subversive' literature.

Even when we eventually got to Tbilisi the problems were not over. The hotel probably wouldn't rate more than two stars in this country; communications with England were near impossible; the food would be rejected in a soup-kitchen; and we had to contend with a noisy 4 a.m. demonstration outside the hotel by Dynamo fans, which interrupted the players' sleep.

It was no way to prepare for a match so finely balanced but, right from the start, there was nothing we could do about it. As in Turkey, it was a question of grin and bear it, and try to produce the answer where it counts - on the field.

This time, however, we were unable to do it. We held on to a goal-less scoreline until half-time, but then lost to three second-half goals which meant that for the second year running we'd gone out in the first round. It was hard to take and, after the costs of the 7,000-mile round trip, it was also financially unrewarding. This was how I summed up: 'As we were aware, our 2-1 lead from the first leg would be difficult to defend, but for fifty minutes we controlled the game. But just when their heads were about to go down they got the breakthrough. Had we taken a similar chance, just before the interval, we would still have been in the cup. As it is we are knocked out for the second year running. It's very disappointing.'

Forest went on to keep the trophy in England, and the following summer in Zurich we finally got the luck of the draw which had deserted us in the two previous years. After winning the League again to qualify once more for Europe's most prestigious tournament, we were paired with Oulun Palloseura, the Finnish team who have the distinction of being the most northerly club in UEFA competitions. It is on the fringe of Lapland, fewer than a hundred miles south of the Arctic Circle, but we didn't anticipate too many problems because the Finns have never exactly been a major force in club football on the Continent.

The first leg was played in Oulu, a small port at the north of the Gulf of Bothnia, in mid-September, not many weeks before the Arctic winter sets in. In such remote parts of Europe you have to fall in with local customs, but some of our club directors were a little bit taken aback when, after being entertained hospitably by their hosts, they were taken to a shore-side sauna where the cold plunge afterwards was into the near-freezing waters of a lake.

As for the match, we drew 1–1 in a small stadium surrounded by a running track and where one touchline had a kink in it – to accommodate the long-jump pit. I wrote: 'On a tight bumpy ground we played a team of part-timers and although we only drew we missed many chances.'

The return at Anfield was a formality, and with Terry McDermott and Graeme Souness each scoring hat-tricks we won 10–1 to go through comfortably to a second-round tie with Aberdeen. 'As the score suggests, this was a cruise,' I recorded.

We knew we were in for a much tougher game in the 'granite city' than we had faced in Finland, but the lads produced a marvellously disciplined performance which was crowned by a delicate first-half chip from an incredibly narrow angle by Terry McDermott, which sent us back to Anfield with the cushion of a one-goal lead for the return.

I noted: 'It was one of our most efficient away games this season, in fact in this competition. Aberdeen proved a useful side with lots of enthusiasm, and the second leg should be another hard game.'

In the return the tie was finished to all intents and purposes by half-time when we led 2–0, and 3–0 on aggregate, and a couple more goals in the second half gave us a 5–0 win overall. 'This was an excellent performance,' I said. 'Aberdeen held out fairly comfortably for twenty-five minutes, chiefly because we seemed to be a bit tensed up. Once we had scored, however, through an own goal from Willie Miller, we played some superb football to which Aberdeen had no answer.'

In seventeen years in Europe we had never played a Bulgarian team, but that was our next stop. The first leg against the country's army team, CSKA Sofia, was, however, at Anfield and came only ten days before we were due to play West Ham at Wembley in the League Cup Final. Incredibly we ran up a 5–1 lead against the Bulgars with Graeme Souness contributing his second hat-trick of the European Cup campaign with some lethal long-range shooting.

'It was one of our best performances, effort-wise,' I wrote in my diary. 'Sofia are a very good side and we will need the cushion. We took our chances at both ends and although they missed a couple, Kenny Dalglish missed the chance of the night. It was a very good result, but it was a blow that Phil Thompson pulled a thigh muscle and must be doubtful for the League Cup Final.'

Phil did, indeed, miss the League Cup Final, which we drew at Wembley, and we were also without Terry McDermott, David Fairclough and Kevin Sheedy as we flew for the first time ever to Bulgaria for the return.

The Levski Stadium may not be as spectacular in its size and design as grounds like the Nou Camp in Barcelona, the Bernabeu Stadium in Madrid, the San Siro in Milan or the World Cup stadiums in Germany, but it has the impressive backcloth of a 7,000-foot mountain, Mount Vitosha, towering above it. The Bulgarians must have thought that represented the size of their task for David Johnson took advantage of a rebound off a post to give us an early lead in the second leg, leaving CSKA needing to score five even to force extra time.

It was a mountain they were incapable of climbing and, in fact, with Ray Clemence saving a penalty, they didn't manage to score even one, and I noted: 'It was an excellent, disciplined performance and when our goal went in around the ten-minute mark it finished them off. But we are not without our injury problems, for David Johnson, Kenny Dalglish, Alan Kennedy and Steve Heighway all received bad knocks and, with Phil Thompson, Terry McDermott, David Fairclough and Kevin Sheedy already out, it does not look promising for the Everton game on Saturday. Just a thought on Sofia: when they had to force their game to get the required goals they didn't look nearly the same side as they did at Anfield.'

It was to be a year later in the same stadium that I fully realised the accuracy of that judgement.

In fact, despite our problems, we managed to beat Everton 1–0 in the Mersey derby on the Saturday, and ten days later won the League Cup – for the first time in Liverpool's history – with a 2–1 replay win over West Ham at Villa Park. That automatically qualified us for Europe the following season but it didn't mean the end of our ambition to win the European Cup for a third time which would rank us alongside such legendary teams as Real Madrid, Ajax and Bayern Munich, the only teams to have won it three or more times.

And it was none other than Bayern who were placed as our last hurdle in our path to the final. After our battles in the old Fairs Cup and the European Cup Winners' Cup some ten years earlier, the overall score was one apiece and we knew we had one helluva match on our hands, particularly with Paul Breitner masterminding the German operation. For the first leg at Anfield we were without David Johnson and Graeme Souness, so Ian Rush was given his first taste of European football with us.

Unfortunately we could only draw 0–0 and, somewhat depressed the next morning, I wrote: 'It was a very disappointing result. Bayern closed the game down, and we didn't have the experience in the side to break them down. With Ray Kennedy needing an injection in his knee, and Graeme Souness and David Johnson out of it, it was asking a lot of youngsters at this level, especially when Terry McDermott dislocated his thumb in the first five minutes and was in such pain that he had to be substituted at half-time. Now we have a tremendous task on our hands, so let's hope we can get our full squad fit in time. We are due a bit of luck.'

Apart from that night in Rome four years earlier, I don't think I have ever been so proud of a team as I was in the Olympic Stadium in Munich a fortnight later. They did me, Merseyside and England proud, and that bit of luck I'd wanted was there in Ray Kennedy, a man whose ability was appreciated far more in Europe than it was in England. At the end of the day we drew the second leg 1–1 to go through to the final in Paris on the away goals rule, but it was Ray who kept his cool to get us there. With only a few minutes left, David Johnson broke on the right and Ray saw the opportunity to get forward. When the centre came over he took his time, turned and tucked the ball deliberately into the net, when many top-class strikers would have whacked the ball first time and probably wasted the opportunity.

Karl-Heinz Rummenigge snatched an equaliser a few seconds from the end but by then it was all over and we were bound for Paris for our third European Cup Final. But I can't leave the story of that night in Munich without mentioning one player – Sammy Lee. It was very rare for Liverpool to single out individual opponents for special attention, because we preferred to let them worry about us, but that night I asked Sammy to do a specific marking job on Breitner. He did it superbly and I shall never forget the cameo in the dressing-room corridor afterwards when Breitner was being interviewed by the Press and Sammy walked past. 'Well played,' said the German star. 'Thank you, Mr Breitner,' said Sammy, humbly.

Naturally, it was a champagne flight back to Speke, for we were on our way to Paris and a showdown in the final with one of the most legendary club teams of all time – Real Madrid, whom we had never met in European competition. But I was at my desk the next morning recording an historic night.

The diary entry read: 'This was possibly our best ever European performance.' I wrote: 'This was the result we were looking for because we contained them and were thoughtful in everything we did. Everything was stacked against us. Phil Thompson failed a fitness test and Kenny Dalglish was kicked out of it in the first three or four minutes, but everyone responded to the task and we finished up deserved winners of the tie. Let's hope we can do it in Paris.'

A thunderstorm, and lightning which struck our plane on its approach to Orly airport, greeted our arrival in the French capital. We stayed outside the city at Versailles, next door to the famous palace with its breathtaking beauty, its Grand Canal, ornamental gardens, fountains and extensive wooded grounds.

The tranquillity was ideal before such a super-charged, emotional occasion like a European Cup Final. The only problem was that the Parc des Princes, France's equivalent of Wembley, is all-seated and has a capacity of only fifty thousand. Paris is within such easy reach of England that we could have filled the stadium with our own fans, but I know a lot were disappointed that they were unable to get tickets to be there to support us that night.

By and large our injury problems had cleared up. At least we were able to field a full strength squad against a Madrid team I had watched in a friendly against Nottingham Forest in the Bernabeu stadium a couple of weeks earlier, but several players were less than one hundred per cent fit. I was under no illusions about how the game would go, and I never thought it would be the classic which everyone was predicting.

My diary states: 'It was a very physical first half and some of the Real Madrid tackling was outrageous, to say the least, but at the same time they had players of real quality. We started quite well but we were upset, probably, by some of the tackles. After the interval we settled down and were well worth our victory, which made British history as we became the first club from these shores to win the Cup three times.'

The man who made history that night, of course, was Alan Kennedy. Who will ever forget him collecting that throw-in from Ray Kennedy, forcing his way past a couple of challenges and, from a seemingly impossible angle, blasting the ball into the net? It was Alan at his unpredictable best, for I'd swear that half the time he doesn't even know himself what he's going to do next!

Without any disrespect, I'm sure he would know what I mean if I say he is not a typical Liverpool player. While he has enthusiasm and heart in abundance and is committed to the cause of the team, he is not the type of player who sees a move three or four passes in advance. He is the instinctive, rather than the calculating type, who reacts to situations rather than creates them. And that's just what he did in Paris.

Rome, London and Paris. Arguably the three most romantic capitals in Europe, and what better places to win three European Cups?

But the arm of coincidence is long, and when almost four months later we set out again in defence of the trophy, we were back to the far north, to Finland, and to Oulu. We'd had the luck of the draw again because, short of absolute disaster, we were guaranteed a place in the second round.

It proved to be almost a repeat of the previous year, as we gained a 1–0 win over there, thanks to a goal by Kenny Dalglish, and crushed the part-time Finns 7–0 in the return at Anfield. This time they didn't have even the consolation of scoring a couple of goals against us.

I recalled: 'The first leg was practically a repeat of last season although we created more chances and worked hard. We still had no luck with our finishing but, like last season, it was not a particularly good game to watch.' Two weeks later I was writing: 'After a slap-happy first half we got to grips with the game and finished off a poor side.'

We were not so lucky with the draw in the second round, however, as we were paired with the powerful Dutch champions, AZ 67 of Alkmaar, who boasted such renowned players as Peters, Metgod Kist and Hovenkamp, and I took the first opportunity of a trip to Holland to watch them against Feyenoord in the same Rotterdam stadium which had been earmarked for the European Cup Final.

I saw enough to know that we would be really put to the test but, once again, we proved our mettle in Europe only to let ourselves down. We built up a two-goal lead in the first leg in Amsterdam, thanks to David Johnson and Sammy Lee, only to squander such a solid advantage by slack play in the closing minutes.

My verdict was: 'It was a repeat of our game at Brighton on Saturday, where we conceded late goals. For an hour we played some of our best football in Europe, and made a good side look very moderate until we conceded two late goals from defensive blunders. Alan Hansen, Phil Thompson and Phil Neal were the culprits, and now we've got it all to do in the second leg.'

Without wishing to be wise after the event, that conclusion was correct, for we managed to win the second leg by only 3–2, to qualify for the quarter-finals in the Spring, and again we were our own worst enemies.

'As anticipated it was a real scrap, but possibly the blame was in our own hands. We had the chances to make the game safe, and when we didn't take them we gave away silly goals, although the first should have been disallowed for off-side. Let's hope we can get our house in order before March,' were my final thoughts on that tie.

I've already mentioned coincidence and I've seen it happen too often in my career to have been surprised when we were drawn, for the second year running in the quarter-finals, with CSKA Sofia. It was back to the Levski Stadium and the awesome sight of Mount Vitosha.

This time, however, the Bulgarians were to prove a peak we could not scale, and there were a number of reasons for it. The first of them was that the first leg at Anfield was played in a strong wind which, on our worn pitch, made it difficult to get our game together. At the same time, as I had noted a year before, the Bulgarians were a useful side, capable of giving anybody a game. As it turned out we could manage only a 1-0 win at Anfield in the first leg, thanks to a goal from Ronnie Whelan, who had made tremendous strides to establish himself both in the First Division and the international arena at a very tender age.

'We didn't get the score we required to make it easy in Bulgaria,' I wrote, 'but it was not for lack of effort. The wind didn't help, but we kept a clean sheet and now it's a lead we must defend.'

We were all confident we could do just that - until we saw the way things were going in the Levski Stadium. And it was not CSKA who were giving us problems, but the Austrian referee, Frans Woehrer. Memories of the San Siro Stadium, Inter-Milan and Senor Mendibil in 1965 flooded back as I watched the decisions being made on that Bulgarian pitch. Ian Rush, who like Ronnie Whelan had emerged as a youngster of outstanding potential, beat the goalkeeper with a header and, as he turned away acclaiming the goal which would surely have clinched it for us, the goalkeeper clawed the ball out of the net and the referee waved play on.

We had also been denied by the woodwork, and the local crowd were booing their team because they hadn't even given our goalkeeper, Bruce Grobbelaar, a shot of note to save. Despite all the problems we were having with the referee, we looked to be on our way to a goal-less draw and a place in the last four until Bruce made a mistake which I'm sure will haunt him for a long time. I would certainly not wish to castigate him for the error, because he was thrust into our first team with no experience of First Division football, never mind the European Cup scene. He didn't have the advantage given to his predecessor, Ray Clemence, of learning the trade for a few years in our reserves, and his error that night in Bulgaria was born out of that inexperience and a lack of understanding with his fellow defenders. He came for a deep cross from the left, which he should never have come for and never had a chance of catching. As a result, not only was he left stranded, but his action put off other defenders who might otherwise have made an effective challenge on Mladenov, who was allowed a free header into an empty net.

It was only about ten minutes from the end and made extra time a sinister prospect. Then, three minutes from the end of normal time, CSKA's dangerous winger, Yonchev, fouled Mark Lawrenson off the ball and Mark appeared to retaliate. He swears he never touched the Bulgarian, but Yonchev collapsed like a sack of spuds, the linesman flagged, and the referee, still twenty-five yards away and without consulting the linesman, produced the red card and Mark became the first player we had ever had sent off in eighteen years of European competition.

I thought it scandalous, and I hope the UEFA representative at the game made an honest report to his superiors in Berne, for there have been too many incidents like this in Europe over the years.

It left us to face extra time with only ten men. Also Terry McDermott was off injured and, as the tackles became more cynical by the minute, I feared the worst. It duly came when Mladinov scored again, and we were out of the European Cup. Our dream of winning it for a fourth time had vanished in the frosty night air of Sofia, and gloomily I recorded: 'This was another disappointing result in a game we should never have lost. We dominated the match and didn't deserve to lose, and even though we were handicapped by poor officials we gave away a silly goal in the last ten minutes which took us into extra time. We hit the woodwork three times but nothing went right for us.'

However, four days earlier we had won the League Cup Final at Wembley against Spurs so at least we were assured of another campaign in one of the European competitions. But there is nothing like adversity to inspire Liverpool, and we set to work to win the League title again to qualify us for the big one – the European Cup.

6 Keegan and Dalglish

Kevin Keegan and Kenny Dalglish are both world class players in their own right, and each has played an immeasurable part in the success of Liverpool. But whenever I hear Kevin's name mentioned, the first feeling I get is a chill down my spine, because he was at the centre of the biggest crisis I ever had to deal with as manager. Indeed, a few turbulent weeks in the late summer and autumn of 1974 could have ended my managerial career almost before it had started, and could have forced Kevin to quit football long before he had climbed to the dizzy heights he reached later.

It was a test of nerve and determination for both of us, and when I reflect on it now, my first steps as manager after succeeding Bill Shankly at the start of the 1974–75 season were about as easy as walking blindfold through a minefield. I even had to contend with Government interference that contributed to making a difficult job almost impossible.

It all began with Bill Shankly's shock decision to retire in mid-July. The announcement stunned the football world almost as much as it did everyone at Anfield. But with a new season dawning, when we were once again challenging in Europe in the Cup Winners Cup, it was essential to keep as much continuity as possible.

By the time we flew out to West Germany in early August for a pre-season conditioning game against Kaiserslautern, I had been appointed Bill's successor, and was to take up my duties officially after the FA Charity Shield game against Leeds and the Billy McNeill Testimonial game against Celtic in Glasgow, which was to be Bill's farewell. But it had already been agreed that I would be in charge of the team for these three pre-season games – and there were problems in the first match against Kaiserslautern.

One of the German players went in dangerously on Ray Kennedy and several of our lads reacted angrily, with the result that referee Gunter Quindeau gave Kevin Keegan his marching orders.

I had to think quickly. If the sending-off was reported to the FA in London, then Kevin could have faced a suspension, which was something I obviously wanted to avoid. So I told Peter Cormack that *he* had been the culprit, not Kevin, and pleaded a case of mistaken identity. We stuck so firmly to the story that we even had Kevin and Peter believing it! As it happened, our efforts were not really necessary, because the referee could not attend the London hearing of the case and the matter was dropped. Anyway, it was small beer compared to what happened the following Saturday at Wembley when we met Leeds in the Charity Shield.

I am not being wise after the event when I say that I am very dubious about playing this sort of game at Wembley, right at the start of a season when players are not tuned in, either mentally or physically. A Wembley match is an occasion that can play havoc with your emotions, and when players are not at their peak, in mind or body, it doesn't take much for nerves to snap and tempers to flare.

Our meeting with Leeds was the first Charity Shield to be staged at Wembley – a decision taken at short notice by the FA – and the tension soared, simply because of the rivalry between the two clubs. For a decade, Liverpool and Leeds had been neck and neck in winning trophies, and together had dominated English football. It was impossible for either set of players to produce anything but a highly competitive match.

The tragedy was that my worst fears were realised. The timing of the match and the occasion was too much. The game was marred by fouls and niggling until emotions exploded in the second half.

Johnny Giles had already been booked for clouting Kevin Keegan before Billy Bremner and Kevin got involved in another incident when the two players swapped punches. Referee Bob Matthewson ordered them both off – Kevin's second dismissal in five days. And as the pair of them trooped back to the dressing-room, the first British players to be sent off at Wembley, they threw their shirts down on the touchline.

I am the last person to condone that sort of behaviour, but at the same time I still believe the two players were victims of circumstance and that those who sit in judgment, the football establishment if you like, were unjustified in coming down on them like a ton of bricks. The fact that we won the Charity Shield on penalties after a 1-1 draw, could not have been further from my mind as we travelled on to Glasgow for the game with Celtic at Parkhead on the Monday night.

Kevin went back home to Doncaster after his experience at Wembley but linked up with us to play Celtic when Shanks said his farewell, to an amazing salute from the Scots supporters. Next morning I took over the reins officially as Liverpool manager - and I could never have expected what was to follow.

After we had won our opening League game at Luton we were to lose Kevin for three matches - his punishment for being sent off at Wembley. But much worse was to come.

Without Kevin in the team, we took three points off Wolves, two at home and one away, and beat Leicester. But the day after our home win over Wolves, I had to accompany Kevin to the hearing by the FA Disciplinary Commission of the charge that both he and Bremner had brought the game into disrepute by throwing down their shirts at Wembley.

The three-man commission was chaired by Vernon Stokes, sitting with Sir Matt Busby and former Aston Villa chairman Norman Smith, and at the end of the hearing I wasn't quite sure whether I was white-faced with anger or disbelief. They slapped a ban on Kevin and Bremner until 30 September, and fined each of them £500. It meant that, in total, Kevin was to miss eleven games for what happened at Wembley - three for being sent off and a further *eight* for the disrepute charge.

I was seething, and Kevin was bitterly upset, angry and disillusioned at the way he had been treated. What rubbed salt in the wound was that we were told there was no appeal against the commission's verdict and that there had been direct Home Office pressure brought to bear on the case.

The serious problem of soccer hooliganism and violence had reared its ugly head again and one fan had been stabbed to death at Bloomfield Road in Blackpool's game with Bolton the previous Saturday. From many quarters had come the cry that examples should be made of Keegan and Bremner. Clearly the Home Office were caught up in the hysteria, for they demanded – and got – what I consider a savage, six-fold sentence on Kevin consisting of:

1 His three-match suspension
2 A club fine which we had been *advised* to impose by the FA
3 An FA fine
4 A further eight-match ban
5 His name blackened throughout the country
6 The denial of his talents to the fans.

It proved to me, once again, that people sitting in judgment are often guilty of giving little thought to the players they expect to provide entertainment. And when those people are former players they have even more to answer for, because they should know better. They seem to think players are machines who can turn it on and off like robots. Yet when players show they are, indeed, only human – which was the sole reason for what happened at Wembley – the FA, and those in Government in this case, show about as much compassion and understanding as the Spanish Inquisition.

It is all very well for people sitting cool, calm and collected in a stand seat, but it's entirely different for a player on a hot day at Wembley before the season has even started. His head is doubtless buzzing with exhaustion, he is wondering where the next breath is coming from, and working himself into a frenzy. The atmosphere can whip a player into a state of near insanity when he isn't properly prepared, and therefore he has little resistance to provocation such as Kevin suffered.

Kevin's father Joe, a former miner who was born just a few yards from my father in the Durham village of Hetton le Hole, was as upset as anyone over the suspension. Joe and I had a good relationship, but he felt I could have done more on Kevin's behalf at the hearing. But the fact was that the case had been virtually pre-judged. There was nothing we could do about it – not even if Petrocelli or Perry Mason had been acting for us.

The next, massive headache was how Kevin would react to his long period of enforced inactivity. After only a few weeks as a manager I knew the situation called for the most tactful psychology. Kevin's fate, mine, and above all, the club's, were all bound up in the outcome. I was convinced that if he trained during that period without being able to play in matches it would kill his enthusiasm for the game. And knowing how deeply Kevin felt about things, there was every chance he would just quit football.

We had a long talk and I suggested he took a month's holiday, to go away somewhere to relax and take his mind completely off the events. First of all he went on a golfing trip to Bournemouth and then went back to Doncaster to see his parents. The next thing he decided to do was music to my ears. 'I think I'll get married,' he told me.

In normal circumstances, you tend to discourage players from marrying in the football season. It is a personal upheaval that is bound to affect their form. But in Kevin's case, it was the silver lining to a very dark cloud. It would happen at an ideal time and lift his spirits as well. So, by the time he was eligible to play for us again he had married his fiancée, Jean – and I had another problem.

During Kevin's absence, the team had made a blistering start to the season, taking eleven points from the opening six games and overwhelming Norwegian side Stromsgodset 11–0 in the first leg of the European Cup Winners' Cup. Phil Boersma and Ray Kennedy had formed an effective spearhead up front and people were even daring me to leave Kevin out of the side. But I knew that, for the sake of the club and my own future as manager, Kevin had to be brought back into the team which had already lost defender Phil Thompson with an injury that led to a cartilage operation.

As if to prove that fate was conspiring against us, Thompson's injury came only a month after I had sold Larry Lloyd to Coventry for what was then a massive fee of £240,000. I was reluctant to part with him, and had put that price tag on his head to scare off prospective buyers. But when Coventry offered to meet it we couldn't refuse. So, with Thompson's injury following Lloyd's departure I had to call on that great clubman, Chris Lawler, to fill the gap in the centre of our defence, even though he was well past his peak.

Our good run was checked by three defeats in four League games, which saw us lose at Manchester City and Sheffield United and at home to Burnley and I brought Kevin straight back into the team for the return leg with Stromsgodset of Norway. He partnered Ray Kennedy and Steve Heighway up front with Phil Boersma switching to midfield. We won 1–0, for what it was worth, giving us an aggregate of 12–0. It was a gentle return for Kevin – but he was back, and I was truly thankful for that.

Before Christmas, Kevin was re-united in our attack with John Toshack, who had himself been through a traumatic period when his proposed transfer to Leicester City fell through on medical grounds. John's problem, as I knew, was caused by calcification in a thigh muscle, which restricted the number of games he could play and was to plague him for the rest of his career.

It was a desperately frustrating first season for me as manager. We went out of the Cup Winners' Cup to Ferencvaros of Hungary in the second round on the away goals rule, and then lost 1–0 at home to Middlesbrough in the fourth round of the League Cup – both during Thompson's absence from the defence. And in the Championship we finished runners-up, two points behind Derby County. At most clubs that would be considered success. But not at Anfield, where the standards and expectancy are sky-high. Perhaps if fortune had been a little kinder to us, and if I'd have had more experience of being in charge, it might have made that crucial difference.

Nevertheless, I was truly thankful that Keegan and Toshack, both of whom could have left the club that season, had re-established their attacking partnership and ended up as our top League goal-scorers with ten and twelve goals respectively. It laid the foundations for the success that was to follow – the League and UEFA Cup double in 1975–76, and the League and European Cup double a year later in 1976–77.

Joe Mercer called Keegan and Toshack the finest attacking combination since John Charles and Sivori at Juventus. They were certainly a potent pair - Kevin, darting, skilful, strong as an ox and super-fit; Tosh, lanky, lethal in the air, yet skilled on the floor for a big man. The great pity for Tosh was that he was restricted by his thigh condition and was unable to play as often as he wished. There were times when he was unhappy at being told he couldn't play in a particular match because of his thigh. That is the natural reaction of most players. But after John became a manager himself at Swansea he told me he now understood that we had had to be careful not to take foolish risks with him.

Nevertheless, he and Kevin scored almost two hundred senior goals for Liverpool between them and, as often happens in football, they came together by sheer accident.

We signed John from Cardiff City for £111,000 in November 1970, but Kevin's arrival the following May was completely overshadowed by events. He came to sign the transfer forms from Scunthorpe just a few days before we met Arsenal in the 1971 FA Cup Final, and because Anfield was then in the throes of modernisation - a rebuilding programme paid for by our years in Europe - he sat on a dustbin in the car park waiting to get into the ground.

We had had several reports on Kevin, including one from our chief scout Geoff Twentyman, and it was late in the season when Bill Shankly asked me and Joe Fagan to have a look at him and give our opinion.

Liverpool had been tipped off about him by Andy Beattie, who was scouting for us, and several League clubs had been interested. Coventry had apparently considered Kevin too small, and Everton had also had a look. But when Joe and I went to see him play in a midweek game for Scunthorpe we did so in the knowledge that Bobby Robson was on the verge of signing him for Ipswich.

Kevin was captain that night, and we saw enough in twenty minutes to convince us that at £35,000 he would be a sound investment. The money would be lost in tax anyway - that was our view then and now, and one I am sure shared by most big clubs.

So the deal was duly completed. But I didn't see much more of

Kevin until shortly before the start of the following season. The day before the Cup Final I did my cartilage in the team's pre-Wembley training session at Hendon, and after the game – which we lost 2–1 after extra time – I came home and went straight into hospital for an operation, so I missed the tour to Scandinavia later that summer in which Kevin was given a free role in the team and scored a goal.

He had played up front for Scunthorpe, but we had viewed him as a prospective midfield replacement for Ian Callaghan, who was getting no younger and had been struggling to recover his form and sharpness after a cartilage operation. Ian had been a wonderful servant to the club, first as a direct, raiding winger through the sixties, and then, after his operation, in midfield. But there had been games when the crowd gave him stick and, knowing Ian's make-up – he's a sensitive lad – I thought it might all be too much for him. As events proved, however, we got a double bonus.

In our pre-season training Kevin looked impressive playing in the attack, and I remember Bill Shankly talking to him in the manager's office at our Melwood training ground just before the season opened. 'How would you like to play up front in our opening game against Nottingham Forest?' he asked Kevin. And Kevin leapt at the chance.

He played in the attack with Toshack and scored on his début in our 3–1 win. Callaghan missed that match but came back for the midweek game against Wolves and was an ever-present for the rest of the season, playing in central midfield. Ian, in fact, went on to play for another seven seasons and performed better than ever. These are the breaks that you are always thankful for in football.

Kevin played outstandingly in his opening seven or eight games, and then complained of a foot injury which was – and still is – a complete mystery.

The one thing Bill Shankly didn't like was an injured player, and Kevin got wind of the fact that Bill had called him a 'malingerer'. It was not said with malice aforethought – it was just Bill being Bill. But Kevin took offence at it and his strong, determined nature was evident even then. I think he was ready to pack up football on the spot. Thankfully, that danger passed and when I examined his foot, and the side of his leg which was also affected, I was baffled as to the cause. We even suspected that a stiff clutch in his car could have been responsible.

Kevin missed several games but one Thursday I took him to a specialist who gave him an injection. Fortunately, it did the trick – and Kevin played on the Saturday.

Apart from a muscle-splitting whack on the thigh he sustained in a game against Dynamo Berlin eighteen months later, Kevin was remarkably free of injuries after that. He had done weight training at Scunthorpe and was exceptionally fit. In fact, he's one of the fittest lads I've ever seen in football.

Kevin made rapid progress in his first season, winning England Under-23 caps and proving a big success on the Under-23 tour the following summer. But, for the club, it was a frustrating season. We had made a run from tenth place and took twenty-eight points from sixteen games before going to Arsenal in the final match needing a win to become champions. Derby had already completed their programme with fifty-eight points, while Leeds, a point behind them with a superior goal average, needed only a draw in their last match at Wolves.

Both Leeds, who had beaten Arsenal to win the FA Cup on the previous Saturday, and ourselves played our last game on the Monday night. Leeds lost, and we were held to a goal-less draw to finish third, a point behind Derby. To add to our frustration John Toshack had the ball in the net but it was ruled off-side. If the goal had been given, we would have been champions!

There was ample compensation the following season of 1972–73, when Keegan and Toshack spearheaded our double success of League championship and UEFA Cup – the club's first European trophy after competing in an unbroken run since 1964. Keegan hit fourteen goals in forty-one League games, and Toshack thirteen in twenty-one First Division appearances, as we won the title with sixty points – three ahead of Arsenal!

The pair of them made crucial contributions to our UEFA Cup triumph. The first leg of the final against Borussia Moenchengladbach was abandoned after twenty-seven minutes with the Anfield pitch flooded. It was replayed twenty-four hours later and Bill

Shankly made one important team change – bringing in Toshack in place of little Brian Hall. The move paid off because Tosh caused the Germans all sorts of problems in the air and Keegan scored twice in our 3–0 win. Although Borussia had pulled back two of the goals by half-time in the second leg they virtually ran themselves out in the process and we came through as 3–2 winners.

A year later we were in another final, the FA Cup at Wembley against Newcastle, and another complete team performance saw Kevin starring again and scoring twice in our 3–0 win.

A few months later came Bill Shankly's decision to retire and after my personal disappointment at finishing only runners-up in the First Division in my first season in charge, I found football history repeating itself for me and Liverpool.

Back in the 1946–47 season, I made thirty-three appearances at left-half in the Liverpool team that won the championship after winning 2–1 at Wolves in the last match at the end of May. And in the 1975–76 season, my second as manager, the club's last League game was again at Molineux, in May, and again the destination of the championship depended on the result.

Queen's Park Rangers had completed their programme and were on top with fifty-nine points. That meant we had to beat Wolves to take the title by a point or gain a low-scoring draw to become champions on goal average. With only fourteen minutes left, we were still trailing to a first-half goal by Steve Kindon, even though we were playing a strong attacking game. Then Kevin met a flicked header from Tosh to shoot the equaliser and we went on to win the championship in style with further goals from Tosh and Ray Kennedy.

A fortnight later, Kevin scored another vital goal for us from a swerving free kick in Belgium to give us a 1–1 draw against Bruges and a 4–3 aggregate win in the second leg of the UEFA Cup Final.

That League and UEFA Cup double compensated for the disappointment I had felt the previous season, and the championship brought us another tilt at the European Cup which we had first set out to win in the 1964–65 season, our first in Europe. Indeed, we might have won it at the first attempt but for the inexperience against the crafty Italians of Inter Milan in the semi-final. We were just greenhorns compared to Inter, and allegations of corruption in that match have rumbled ever since.

There were problems from the Continent of a different kind before the 1976–77 season opened. The Europeans began to cast their envious eyes on Kevin, who was the reigning Footballer of the Year and had already had the honour of captaining England under Don Revie's management. Kevin announced that he wanted a fresh challenge, that he wanted to try his luck abroad. The Press, radio and television were full of it. Barcelona had already shown interest when the Liverpool chairman John Smith and I went to Heathrow Airport in the summer to meet Real Madrid officials.

At the time, Kevin was in Northampton General Hospital recovering from a fall off a bicycle in a TV *Super Stars* competition. But we kept him fully aware of developments in frank and friendly discussions. Real Madrid were ready to pay £650,000 for him, but we obviously wanted to keep him. Kevin's reaction was that he wanted to have a crack at helping Liverpool win the European Cup, and we in turn assured him that he would be kept fully informed of any enquiries for him and that we would let him go at the end of the season if the right offer came in.

It was a gentleman's agreement, and my own feeling was that if we got another sparkling season from Kevin it would only be for the good of the club. However, the interest from abroad had come a little too soon because it affected the whole of Kevin's season. Even though I was sure that any foreign clubs interested in Kevin would keep such close tabs on him they'd know what he ate for breakfast, lunch and dinner, the situation worried Kevin and got on top of him.

He was constantly wondering who would come in for him and when. Eventually, it even caused Kevin and sections of our supporters to get at loggerheads. He was frustrated and the crowd were angry that they were going to lose the greatest player in the country, a player they loved and virtually worshipped.

In the middle of that 1976–77 season Kevin suffered the tragic loss of his father, Joe, in December. They had been very close, and

Joe's death deeply upset Kevin. So with all his personal turmoil it was not surprising that we didn't see the best of him that season.

Nevertheless, we won the League title, and Kevin finished as top scorer with 12 goals. But the great achievement was our long-awaited European Cup triumph in Rome, when we beat Borussia Moenchengladbach 3–1.

By then, Kevin was bound for Hamburg and he produced a magnificent personal performance in the Olympic Stadium. His determined run late in the game forced that great West German defender, Berti Vogts, to send him sprawling for the clinching goal from the penalty spot by Phil Neal. It was Kevin's farewell appearance and he went out in a blaze of glory. He was outstanding, but, five days earlier at Wembley, he had been only a shadow of his usual self as we lost the FA Cup Final to Manchester United.

Perhaps in different circumstances we would have seen the best of Kevin on both occasions and become the first English club to win the treble of League championship, FA Cup and the European Cup. But that must remain in the category of what might have been.

On the day Kevin signed for Hamburg in a London hotel for £500,000 I said that no player who leaves this country to play abroad should be picked for England – and the remark was quoted in next morning's newspapers. Some time later, Kevin said in an article that he could never forgive me for saying that. But I did not make it as a personal comment aimed at Kevin, because I have always had the utmost admiration for him. He is courageous as well as skilled, and he is made of the same village stuff as me. I said it because I was concerned at losing our best players abroad. It was the British football public I was concerned about because it is they who suffer if they are deprived of seeing our star players in action week after week. There is also the problem of British players abroad having to be released by their clubs for our international matches. There has got to be an understanding hammered out by UEFA and the Common Market over this matter, because some countries are still stubborn on this issue.

It was only a few years ago that English clubs *had* to release players for England, but could make up their own minds on whether to release their men for Scotland, Ireland or Wales. Then it was agreed that they must all be treated alike. This must now be extended to cover the whole of Europe.

Kevin, of course, repeatedly stressed his desire to play for England and insisted on a release clause in his contract with Hamburg, and what I said was not meant to be detrimental to him.

I had some difficulties with him, more than Bill Shankly had when he was manager, because under Shanks I saw a major part of my job as keeping trouble out of his office and nipping any problems in the bud. I am talking about situations such as the one caused by Kevin's mystery leg injury shortly after his arrival at Liverpool. That called for the utmost tact, diplomacy and psychology gained from a lifetime in football. Even when I succeeded Shanks as manager, Kevin and I still had some good, heart to heart talks. When I first took the job on I refused a contract. I said I wanted to do the job and earn one. But Kevin told me that he thought I should have a contract for my own good. I think he thought of me as a father figure. But he was never impudent with me – he never overstepped the mark.

The chat we had after Kevin had walked out on England helped to heal the breach with Don Revie. Kevin came to see me at Anfield, and although I don't condone what he did, I fully understood his motives. On the previous Saturday, Kevin had gone ahead and played for England against Northern Ireland in Belfast despite a death threat which had been made in a letter. But when Don announced the England team for the following Wednesday's game with Wales at Wembley, it did not include Kevin, and what really upset him was that Don did not say a word to him about it. So, eventually, Kevin packed his bags and left the England squad's hotel.

Kevin and I had a talk about the situation and, again, I saw my job was to pick him up and lift his spirits. Don Revie telephoned, we exchanged points of view, and the axe was buried.

Later, of course, Ron Greenwood succeeded Revie as England manager and Kevin's stature as an England player became immense. In his early appearances under Sir Alf Ramsey, I think his role in the team was too rigid. Ideally, Kevin likes to fill attacking roles from wide on the left to the old inside-right berth, but when he started his England career, they wanted him tied down to a position wide on the right. It did not really suit him and, consequently, Kevin's England place was not as secure and automatic as it became later, with the crowning glory of captaining his country.

When he went to West Germany, they said he became a better player, but his role at Hamburg was different from his role at Liverpool. In Germany, clubs give their men marking jobs, asking a player to follow one of the opposition players wherever he goes. We never asked Liverpool players to do that, except in a few exceptional circumstances over the years.

Kevin's departure to Hamburg left me with the headache of replacing him. We had £500,000 in the bank and a big gap in the team. I just hoped that after the trials and tribulations of my early taste of management, someone on high would smile on me and guide my hand.

My plea was answered. We signed Kenny Dalglish from Glasgow Celtic and still had £60,000 left of the income from Kevin's transfer! Just as Kevin had wanted a new challenge, so Kenny had let it be known to Celtic that he was unsettled.

Our relationship with Celtic was always a good one, and they got in touch with Liverpool to see if we would be interested in signing Kenny should he become available. When Celtic made that first contact, I was on holiday in Majorca with Tom Saunders, Liverpool's youth development officer, and the man who vets the club's European opponents. Of course I was interested in Kenny Dalglish – a fine player, tailor-made for a passing team like Liverpool.

I cut short my Spanish holiday and came back home. I told my wife, Jessie, that I would be making myself scarce for a few days. But I didn't even tell her where I was going, because I didn't want it to be public knowledge where I was. Jessie will not tell lies, so if she didn't know where I was going she wouldn't have to tell lies if anyone tried to find me. I promised her I would ring her each night while I was away. My secret hideaway was, in fact, a small hotel in North Wales, and the only person who knew about it was my very good friend, Ray Peers.

It was Ray who told me that Jock Stein had been trying to contact me at the club, and when I rang home, Jessie told me he had left his telephone number. When I spoke to Jock, he told me he was going to make another attempt to persuade Kenny to stay at Parkhead, but asked me whether, if he was still adamant about leaving, we would be in the market for him at around £440,000. The make or break element in the situation was Celtic's looming Australian tour. If Kenny preferred not to go on it, then Jock was resigned to losing him.

I spoke to our board about the matter, and they told me that if Kenny was available, and if he was the player I wanted, I had the go-ahead to sign him. In turn, I informed Jock and also told him that we wanted to sign Kenny before the 15 August deadline for the European Cup, otherwise we would have to look elsewhere to try to replace Kevin.

Celtic left for their Australian trip without Kenny, but when I spoke to Jock by telephone in Singapore he told me he was still going to have another try at persuading him to stay at the club when he got back. Jock and I agreed that, with the European deadline moving closer, Tuesday 9 August must be the day of decision.

Jock kept his word and contacted me on the Tuesday morning. He'd had another chat with Kenny but had failed to persuade him to stay with Celtic, and, reluctantly, he was making him available. He asked us to meet him at Parkhead at ten o'clock that night after Celtic's friendly game at Dunfermline.

I dashed up to Scotland with the Liverpool chairman John Smith, and, in an effort to avoid recognition, we booked into a Moffat hotel as brothers under the assumed names of 'John and Bill Smith'. A few minutes after we had checked in someone came up to me and asked, 'Can I have your autograph, Mr Paisley?' The cover had been quickly blown.

When we arrived at Parkhead we talked with Jock and Kenny, the deal was done in about ten minutes, and he travelled down to sign at Anfield the next day. The £440,000 fee was then a record between two British clubs. It seems ridiculously low now, for Kenny has been a tremendous investment for Liverpool. I said at the signing ceremony that we had bought probably the best player in Britain – a proven goal-scorer with skill to play anywhere. We went for the best without making too much fuss about it – we wanted to get on with the job.

Ironically, Kenny had been at Anfield more than a decade earlier when he came down as a fifteen-year-old for trials. He came twice, and on one of his visits managed to get a ticket to watch the 1966 FA Charity Shield match between champions Liverpool and FA Cup winners Everton at Goodison Park, an occasion made even more historic when Roger Hunt and Ray Wilson carried England's newly won World Cup around the ground.

Apparently, Bill Shankly asked Kenny to come down from Scotland for a third trial but Kenny, who also had trials with West Ham, preferred to stay in Scotland and join Glasgow Celtic. I know that I was delighted that he eventually decided to move south of the border – with good reason, because he has been some performer for Liverpool.

He is a superb professional. His approach to a training match or a five-a-side game is just as keen as it is in a cup final, and his ability to withstand knocks and whacks from defenders is remarkable. Kenny will never put forward excuses, not even in the rare spells when he has not been scoring goals. He always gives his utmost to the team, he always wants to contribute, and yet he has remained so modest about his ability that I have often been tempted to remind him of his own individual skill.

Without missing a match after his transfer, it took him just 101 games to hit fifty goals for Liverpool. It is a feat in itself to play so many consecutive games operating up front in the most demanding role in football. To hit half a century of goals in the process is some achievement.

Typical of his skills was the goal he scored against Bruges in the 1978 European Cup Final at Wembley at the end of his first season. At the angle he was to goal, and the position in which he received the ball, many players would have snatched at the chance, but Kenny's ice-cool football brain delayed the shot until the Bruges keeper, Jensen, had committed himself – then Kenny tucked the ball away.

One of the most frequent questions I am asked is who is the better player – Keegan or Dalglish? But it's so hard to choose between them. They are both greats of the game. I do know one thing – I wish I could have had them both as a manager. It would simply be a question of choosing the other nine players and a substitute and I'd expect to win the Grand National as well as cups and championships.

They are players of contrasting styles. Kevin is a bustling, hustling player who employs his tremendous energy and physique to twist in all directions, whereas Kenny's anticipation allows him to turn players in one smooth movement. Kevin likes to run with the ball and carry it, while Kenny is a purveyor of it. He likes to have people around him so that he can use his vision. Kevin injects a racy tempo with his mobility, Kenny likes to stroke the ball around. The judgement in Kenny's passing bears the hallmark of great golf shots. And he can read ground conditions the way cricketers can. He has the uncanny knack of knowing a ball will bounce, carry or skid on a particular surface.

Both Kevin and Kenny are quick – Kevin is physically faster. Kenny's first five yards are in his head, as John Toshack had the first two yards in his head when he partnered Kevin. Just as Kevin had Tosh, so Kenny formed admirable partnerships, latterly with Ian Rush but first with David Johnson, whose strong running and mobility not only produce goals but also allow him to act as a decoy to move players around and create chances for others. His goals in fact have been a bonus – I always saw Johnson's main task as disturbing defences.

Neither Kevin nor Kenny are outstanding at heading the ball, but they are more than competent in the air, and while Kenny reads what colleagues and opponents do, Kevin reacts to them – two differing techniques.

Because of the differences between Kenny and Kevin, so there was a change in the Liverpool style when Kenny followed Kevin into the team. With Kenny's subtlety, a 4–4–2 formation with the accent on passing was clearly our most effective line-up. But there is no doubt in my mind that Kevin and Kenny would form a lethal blend. Great players can always play together.

When they come to write my epitaph they might say this: Bob Paisley was a successful manager but he was probably the most unfortunate of all, because he never had Keegan and Dalglish in the same Liverpool team.

But if I had to choose one of them, it would have to be Kenny. As individuals he and Kevin are on a par. But Kenny can make a team spark collectively with his gifted ability to read situations, and offers other players so many options with his wide-ranging distribution and vision.

Of all the players I have played alongside, managed and coached in more than forty years at Anfield, he is the most talented. When Kenny shines, the whole team is illuminated.

7 For Club and Country

When Liverpool won the European Cup two years on the trot, a number of prominent managers, both here and abroad, made a point which I had known for some time, yet modesty forbade me from stating it in public. Don Revie, when he left England, said the current Liverpool side would have beaten the national team. Others, particularly Miljan Miljanic, said Liverpool would have been favourites to win the World Cup if we had played in Argentina in 1978.

Those are pretty revealing remarks, but if they had emanated from me it would have made my job that much harder and put even greater pressure on the Liverpool team. The fact that I agree almost entirely with those comments is not the point I am driving at.

If Liverpool were so good at club level, it's difficult to defend the record of our national teams over the same period, and in particular England's.

It's a source of great disappointment to everyone that we have won the World Cup only once, and then with the advantage of playing all our matches at Wembley. I think it's even more disturbing that we didn't even qualify for the finals until 1982. True, we went to Mexico in 1970 as the holders, just as we qualified in 1966 as the hosts, but until 1982 we had been on the outside looking in.

This is a quite ridiculous state of affairs. Considering Liverpool's record in Europe, and Forest's too, there is something sadly wrong somewhere. When Forest kept Europe's top prize in England in 1979, we became the first country, starting with Manchester United of course in the 1960s, to provide three different European

Cup-winning teams.

There have been great sides in the past, notably Real Madrid, Inter Milan, Ajax and Bayern Munich, but England's record now in the European Cup and other UEFA competitions suggests we have the greatest strength in depth of any country.

It is generally agreed that our First Division is the most competitive in the world, and the demand from overseas for television coverage of our games is enormous. The Continentals like to watch our football because it is more exciting and we have more quality teams than they have. So why is it that England have been in the doldrums for so long as an international force, and, to a lesser extent, the other home countries too? There is no easy answer, otherwise Ron Greenwood, Don Revie and Jock Stein would have found it by now.

Being manager of the international team is totally different from running a club side, as Bobby Robson is now finding out. The demands and objectives cannot be compared, and I'm prepared to accept that the pressures are greater, even though no side endured as much as we did, going for the treble of the League title, FA Cup and European Cup in 1977.

Basically there is a common fault in all international teams, and it's hard to see how any manager can solve it because it's all a question of human nature.

Any player picked for his country is anxious to do well in order to win prestige and the chance of representing it again. That's where the trouble starts. Many international players are too interested in safeguarding their own positions - even at the expense of the side. And managers contribute to this. How many times have you read that manager X told his new cap to 'Just go out and play your normal game.' That's the classic case of a manager avoiding his responsibility. If eleven internationals, culled from half a dozen clubs, went out at Wembley and did just that, I shudder to think what the outcome would be - chaos and total disorder, I fancy.

Ron Greenwood's first international team for England is an example. He was thinking on the right lines when he plumped for the club system, and took half the Liverpool side to play against Switzerland. There were howls of criticism even before the game, and a lot more afterwards. The game ended in a 0–0 draw, and I'm still not clear whether the critics were upset because there were so many Liverpool players in the side, or whether they just resented the idea of the national team being based on a club side.

I believe Ron Greenwood was right to go for this approach, but having decided to do so, he should have gone the whole hog. We had a four-man midfield of Case, McDermott, Callaghan and Ray Kennedy, but unfortunately, Ron just played three of them – Case was not selected. The result was a key man in *our* formation was missing, which threw extra work on the other three, and particularly Ian Callaghan, who was playing his first international for eleven years, and that in his testimonial season with Liverpool. Ron knew the strength of our midfield, but it was based on the collective efforts of four men, not three. The result at Wembley was that Ian Callaghan, at thirty-five, was expected to do twice the amount of running he was used to. In our system Case and McDermott did the bulk of the running and Cally was the playmaker.

If Ron had picked the four and said, 'Play your own game', and the plan had still flopped, the critics might have had a legitimate grouse.

I believe a top club side will always be more effective than the national one until the wrinkles are ironed out. There are players in the game today who are more interested in representing their countries than their clubs and this is noticeable, particularly at the start of the season. Some players will protect themselves in League matches to avoid injury if they know an international game is imminent. Again, it may be human nature, but that does not mean we must accept it.

It's not easy to adopt that attitude if you are a Liverpool player, because our game is based on teamwork, and everyone pulling their weight. Any shirker would soon stand out like a sore thumb, because nearly all our matches have something at stake.

But a player with a less successful club, which is not expected to win anything over the season, can coast along in the First Division, and then explode at international level. That's a bonus for the national manager, but if I were that player's club manager, I would want to know why he was not performing at that level for his club – after all, we do pay the wages.

Ron Greenwood later introduced a variation on the club system by sticking as closely as he could to the same squad of players for every game. Again, I can see the logic of this – and the pitfalls. I could never make out a case for including injured players in the squad, far less for selecting men who are not physically fit, and Ron did this in several instances. Against Denmark in September 1979, he included Bob Latchford, who had only played two reserve games all season, Kevin Keegan, who it was widely known was carrying an injury, as well as Trevor Francis, who hadn't played at all since returning from America. Another forward selected, Laurie Cunningham, was unable to obtain his release from Real Madrid.

The result was that Ron was effectively without four of his strikers, yet, rather than disturb his squad, he didn't call up anyone else and went with what he had. In my opinion, that was carrying loyalty too far. There is a vast selection of players in England, and this was an opportunity to bring in a few of them.

A similar situation arose the previous season. Emlyn Hughes was selected for England when he was in Liverpool's reserve team, and the man who had taken his place, Phil Thompson, was overlooked. Later that season, Phil was injured, Emlyn came back into the Liverpool first team, but it was Phil who was picked to play for England! If you find that hard to follow, you are not alone!

Of course there are many other reasons why England are no longer the kings of the game, and for these neither Ron Greenwood nor any England manager is to blame. We are the pioneers, and everyone else has scrutinised our way of playing until they know it backwards. That makes it easier to counter.

British football still has strengths the Continentals will never better, but they have developed their own technique, and in some departments they are ahead of us. Also the game has changed in a way that has not helped British teams. When I played the game I was known as a pretty hard tackler, and there were plenty like me, but tackling has become almost obsolete in the modern game.

The Continentals never liked it and it seems referees now share their opinion. It's a pity, because it's taken away a basic part of football and certainly one of our best features.

You would be surprised how much of a part the weather can play. In this country we get the lot, and it's not conducive to playing skilful football. I believe climate governs the way football is played. The Latin-American clubs are high on skill – they are the sunshine footballers. Pitches remain constant, and because the temperature is higher the game is played at a slower pace, thus putting the emphasis on skill. This was shown to classic effect by Flamengo of Brazil when they beat us 3–0 in the 1981 World Club championship in Tokyo on a surface ideally suited to their 'beach' football.

In Europe, and the north in particular, it's colder and wetter, pitches are heavier, and strength inevitably plays a more important part in the game. That's why we usually beat the South Americans over here, and come unstuck over there. But it's something we can come to terms with.

Liverpool's many years in Europe have meant we have played in all manner of conditions, from near heatwaves in Spain, to ice and snow in Poland. We have kicked off as early as 11 a.m., and on other occasions nearer to midnight. It might upset the routine you are used to, but it does not mean you should use that as an excuse.

A few years back, Liverpool went to Turkey for the first time, and the conditions on and off the pitch were hardly what we were used to. Trabzon, a port on the Black Sea, is a far cry from the tourist's idea of Turkey. We know that Istanbul can cater for the European visitor, but in Trabzon we were not happy with the hotel, or the health risks, and the so-called dressing-rooms would have been rejected by a Sunday afternoon team. The pitch was uneven, with dangerous pot-holes in it, and the crowd was only inches from the touchline, apart from a few hundred perched at the top of some trees.

It would have been easy to surrender, especially as we had hardly eaten or slept throughout our stay in Trabzon, but we survived, losing 1–0 to a penalty, before winning through in the second leg: a tie I have talked about in an earlier chapter. Those were the worst conditions I have ever come across, and it's when you face that kind of thing that you look for the character and spirit in the side. Without it your chances are next to zero.

Of the home countries, England will always have the best chance, and yet, I'm a great believer in the saying that the more choice and knowledge you have in this game, the greater your own doubts.

Scotland produce a different type of player. Skill is high on their list of priorities and so is their ability to produce versatile players. They will always be a threat to England, because, mistakenly, they believe that is *the* fixture of the season. But harnessing that fierce pride to something like the organisation that Wales have managed to produce first under Mike Smith and now Mike England with very limited resources, would make the Scots a better proposition.

8 Change

Jealousy, greed and all the other elements of a power struggle are strangling our national sport in their tentacles at a time when everybody connected with the game should be looking to the future and charting a progressive course into the next century. The horizon is clear enough, but the way to it is littered with obstacles which it will take men of vision, courage and integrity to surmount.

In the last twenty-five years alone, the game in this country has progressed at top level from having just two competitions to having as many as four for the more successful clubs. Back in the middle fifties, the champions Chelsea abided by, but their successors Manchester United defied, a Football League recommendation not to enter a newly-formed competition, the European Cup. Yet, in less than thirty years, it has become the supreme club prize, the bonus for winning the championship, and provides, quite apart from the financial advantages, the opportunity to gain international prestige for both club and country. Well-run clubs like Liverpool, Spurs and Manchester United have carried out major re-building work on their grounds with their profits from successful campaigns in Europe, and if all that can happen in twenty-five years, what, if natural progression continues, will be happening by the year 2000?

Soon, I think we shall see a European League, and then, with supersonic travel, and the emergence on to the football scene of hitherto non-soccer-playing nations, there could even be a World League by the end of the century. But if we are to achieve such lofty ambitions, football in this country must take a long, hard look at itself, its attitudes and its administration and follow the examples being set abroad.

First and foremost we must achieve unity. It is no good going on any longer with two bodies running the game - often pulling against each other. The Football Association, which is the ruling body, and the Football League, which controls the greater part of the professional game, must merge, or not only will we not make progress but we will fall behind the rest of the world.

Let me remind you of just some of the things that could quite easily have been sorted out, but which remained bones of contention. There was the invitation by Uruguay to England to enter the international team in a competition in 1980–81 for past winners of the World Cup. Various ideas were suggested but in the end the blame for England's refusal to participate in the Mundialato was placed on the top clubs concerned, including Liverpool. Why? Because the FA proposed one way in which the mid-season trip to South America could be accommodated, and the League proposed another. They could not agree, yet had it been one body, I don't doubt that the trip could have been arranged.

The League and the clubs concerned would have accepted an interruption in their fixture list if they had been allowed the scope to extend their season. The FA would not agree, refusing either to alter the dates or to cancel for one season the Home Internationals.

Liverpool were also criticised when after their European Cup wins in 1977 and 1978 they refused to take part in the unofficial World Club Championship with the winners of the South American Cup, but there were sound reasons for those refusals.

The first was the lack of encouragement and help from the game's administrators towards a club trying to enhance this country's prestige abroad. They were not prepared to postpone a League match to allow Liverpool to recover from the effects of a trip to the other side of the world.

And secondly, to finance such an operation would mean charging the earth for the leg which was played at Anfield. Later on the Swedish club Malmo caught a cold in this respect when they took Nottingham Forest's place in the competition, for their home gate was a mere five thousand.

Yet the World Club Championship could be made too attractive to ignore if both UEFA and the South American Cup organisers agreed that the winners should automatically be allowed entry the next season into the relevant continental cup. It is the prospect of an early guarantee of European football the following season that has increased the importance of the Milk Cup from an insignificant competition, and indeed an intrusion, into a most prestigious affair.

Incentive and challenge are two of the basic foundations of football and I cannot see any team being able to ignore the World Club Championship if there was a significant reward for winning it.

We finally competed in December 1981, and the reasons were two-fold. Firstly, we obtained the co-operation of Birmingham City in re-arranging a First Division game, scheduled for the Saturday, so that we could fly to Tokyo for a one-off game against Flamengo of Brazil on the Sunday. Without that co-operation we couldn't have accepted, because we would not have been able to fly out in the middle of the previous week and have a couple of days to overcome the effects of jet-leg. Nottingham Forest had found this a problem the previous year when they returned only the day before an FA Cup tie with Bristol City – and almost lost it.

Secondly, sponsorship, and the fact that it was a one-off match in front of a sixty-two thousand crowd in Tokyo, meant that the financial inducements to us were far too great to ignore.

It was wrong of the media to criticise us for not playing previously, because the real culprits were the fixture-planners. Allowances for such things as the World Club Championship or the Mundialato should be made before the season starts, and then we would be able to compete on equal terms with the rest of the world. The fixture-planners could help by postponing the whole programme for a fortnight, and by doing that they would also prevent other teams stealing a psychological march by arranging a game and possibly opening up a lead at the top of the table.

In 1981–82 Spurs found themselves in a terrible position, not dissimilar to the problems we faced in going for a treble in 1977. Perhaps Spurs were even worse off, because they were going for four trophies, but the pressures were just too much for them. In this country we penalise our successful clubs by lacking the foresight to cater for any success they may achieve. How on earth, when England and the other British nations had a chance of qualifying for the World Cup Finals in Spain the following summer and therefore needed all the preparation they could get, did the powers that be decide to start the season two weeks *later* than normal? Surely it would have been common sense to have started it two weeks *earlier* and then some of the problems that were encountered would never have arisen – and Spurs would have had a fairer crack of the whip.

But good old-fashioned common sense is something that has not been very prevalent in our soccer over the last few years, and the crisis which has hit the game has been on the cards for some time. I started this chapter with two words – jealousy and greed – and they sum up the attitudes of men who have caused the crisis. Big businessmen decided to use football as an ego trip, using their wealth to buy shares and become directors and subsequently chairmen. But you cannot run a football club like a mill, steel works or any other industrial business, because the product is not produced by machines. The end product of a game of football is provided by human beings on the field, and that human element was the factor too often ignored.

A few decades ago football was still considered a sport and not a money-making concern. There were only two competitions, which meant fewer games, and there was a maximum wage, which meant that most clubs could survive on what they took at the turnstiles. But people came into the game who thought they could make a killing and things went beserk. Whether those of us, who remember the old days, liked it or not, it became big business with finance playing a major part in it all. I am sure it will sort itself out, but it will need sensible men with the good of the game at heart rather than their own prestige.

We suffered a recession in the late twenties and early thirties which was every bit as bad and probably worse than the latest one, but it didn't have the same effect on football because then the game was still played as a sport. But the effects of the latest recession are almost certain to mean that significant changes will have to be made.

Finance has been the cancer which has been eating the game from within, and the only way to cure it is for everyone to cut his coat according to his cloth. That means living within his means and not spending excessively on transfer fees and wages - or building stadiums that he just can't afford.

I like to think we got it right at Anfield, and other clubs envied us - but we were forced to do it. We were one of the worst sufferers, percentage-wise, from falling gates, mainly because of localised conditions of unemployment, etc., and with a minimum, instead of a maximum, entrance-fee regulation there was little we could do to increase turnstile income. We couldn't charge more because the fans couldn't afford it and we simply weren't allowed to charge less in an attempt to attract more people.

With the aid of sponsorship, souvenirs and substantial guarantees for friendlies or matches such as the World Club Championship, plus economies in various departments of the club, we kept afloat. We wanted to develop the Kemlyn Road side of the ground with a new stand, but that plan had to be shelved indefinitely because we just could not afford it. You shouldn't spend what you haven't got, and we saw the red light. Had we not done so, the future could have seen Liverpool in as sorry a financial plight as the likes of Chelsea and Wolves who went ahead with ambitious building plans without the guarantees of success on the field to help fund the operations.

Here again the authorities could lead the way by insisting that clubs submit their accounts to the League when they are planning such projects, and only giving the go-ahead when the League are satisfied that the club can afford it.

But one of the biggest obstacles to progress is the voting system at League meetings, where a 75 per cent majority is needed to change a rule. Among the innovations I would like to see are a reduction in the number of teams in each division with, say, four divisions of eighteen and one of twenty, which would maintain the current ninety-two-club membership of the League; the lower divisions going part-time; and a 'keep your own' rule about takings instead of the 'Robin Hood' system of the rich subsidising the poor.

A reduction in the number of clubs per division would provide greater flexibility with fixtures in the event of postponements through bad weather and would help clubs who were successful in Europe and other cup competitions. I am also sure that fewer games would increase the quality of our football because it would not be quite the long, hard slog that it is at the moment.

Greater quality would attract more people through the turnstiles and counter the argument, so often put forward, that clubs need all the fixtures they can get because they need the income from the extra gates. Football must give people what they want, and that is greater quality and entertainment. Without that the problems will continue. Physical combat in a sporting manner has got to be the watchword, for that is what the people want.

Part-time football in the lower divisions must surely come, in fairness both to the clubs and to the players. It would help the little clubs to survive on low gates and would also allow what are mainly poorly paid players to use football to supplement a wage from elsewhere instead of football being their only income. The successes of non-League clubs like Altrincham and Scarborough are examples of the benefits of part-time football.

The little clubs too must not be allowed to prevent change by ganging together to block proposals that might eventually be to their benefit. All too often we have been hamstrung in efforts to introduce much-needed reforms by the selfish element of fear. The bigger clubs, with their far greater financial commitments, need to keep their own revenue and not be paying it into pools which ultimately subsidise those who have fallen on hard times because they have thrown away their money irresponsibly.

And these changes, and others which would help football overcome its problems and give it a firmer foundation for the future, could come about if the game was served by one master instead of the present two, the League and the FA.

Sponsorship is another field where there is a discrepancy between the FA and the League. The FA negotiated a contract with the sports firm Admiral to supply the England strip, and the company's name and emblem were emblazoned across television screens whenever there was an international. Yet the contracts for domestic and European matches prevent clubs from displaying shirt advertisements in televised matches.

Then there is the disciplinary side. The League appoint and control the referees, yet it is the FA who hand out the punishments. There are too many of these grey areas where it is unclear who does what, and too often the two bodies pull against each other, to the detriment of the game.

Under the more diplomatic leadership of Ron Greenwood, one thorny problem of the past largely disappeared – that of the conflicting interests of club and country when it came to the release of players for international duty.

One thing, however, that must never be allowed to happen is an all-out war between the League and the FA. They have got to become a unified body, because although the League would be the stronger if it came to war, there would be no winners – and the only loser would be the game itself.

The League, controlling as it does the vast majority of the country's full-time professional players, could ban them from FA representative teams and re-establish its own Football League side in its place. And it could also bar its clubs from entering the FA Cup, which would not only deprive it of all its glamour and excitement, but would also be financially ruinous to the FA.

Such drastic steps must never happen, of course, but to eliminate even the slightest chance of it, the two bodies must merge. The British way of life is democratic, yet that is not always the case in football, for the powerful figures in the two administrations have often appeared to me to be running things as if they were dictators. That is one of the reasons I was always far happier accepting UEFA rulings, because they all come from various committees set up within the organisation.

That European body in more than twenty-five years successfully brought together thirty-four nations of different political creeds and religions into one streamlined body – so why have we not learned the lesson from them?

I would like to see the League and FA merge under a chairman who had integrity, some knowledge of football and a sound business sense, and who enjoyed the respect of people connected with soccer, from the fans to the boardrooms. An inner cabinet, representative of all aspects of the game – managers, referees, players, etc., and not excluding people from the non-professional levels of the game – would then thrash out policy and the problems of the day. Between them they would have the knowledge and experience to go into all aspects of some of the thornier problems which arise, and would be able to point football in the right direction. That would be far more efficient and beneficial than the system which applies in the Football League at the moment, when it needs a 75 per cent majority of the votes to change a rule.

This is where jealousy, fear and greed come in. A proposal to reduce the First Division to eighteen clubs stands little chance of being accepted, because the only ones in favour would be the handful of big ambitious clubs. The limit of some clubs' ambition is to preserve their First Division status, and some even give their players bonuses for avoiding relegation. They would vote against bringing the trap-door four places nearer, and so would the Second Division clubs when they saw their chances of promotion reduced.

Yet it has got to come, just as automatic promotion and relegation through a pyramid system from the very grassroots of local Sunday League football to the First Division has got to come. Football has thrived for a century on ambition and competition, and that has got to be maintained and increased.

The setting up of a new, streamlined, unified body is the top priority. Then they can set about restructuring the game from the bottom – and I mean from the most junior level, the kids of eight or so who show promise.

I would advocate the setting up of special schools at which the development of their football talent would run parallel to their general, academic education. It would not be at the expense of normal education but as an addition to it. The lads would have the benefit of their natural talent being nurtured and developed by expert coaches, and not by ambitious and inexperienced schoolmasters who are less interested in the boy himself than in the prestige to be gained by winning a local schools cup. This can lead to individual expression being sacrificed to team effort.

I know a man whose talents are perfectly suited to masterminding such a scheme – Tom Saunders, Liverpool's Youth Development Officer under my management. He was once a headmaster and used to manage both England Schoolboys and the England Youth teams.

The further development of the youngsters could then be transferred to the professional clubs, which is at present impossible because of the FA restrictions. The current rules often mean that when a youngster is old enough to link up with a professional club, he has already formed too many bad habits which are difficult to eradicate and which often remain with him throughout his career.

That fault in the system alone has prevented many promising youngsters making it to the top. The system I am advocating works in many countries abroad, and I would stress again that it would not be at the expense of a boy's academic education. It is just that natural talent has to be developed and encouraged in the proper way from the time it is first apparent. A budding musician, after all, is encouraged to take tuition from a professional, and the same principle applies to football as much as to music.

Such a system might help overcome one of the less savoury sides of professional football – under-the-counter payments for youngsters. How many times have you read stories about a boy who apparently escaped the scouting net of his local club and was snapped up by another club hundreds of miles away? Often. And sometimes it has something to do with illegal inducements. The top club does not necessarily sign the best youngster, especially if his ambitious and out-of-work father is offered a four- or five-figure cheque and new furniture for his home.

At Liverpool we never did this, never contemplated doing it, and by and large didn't need to. Merseyside has always produced more than its fair share of young football talent, and the ambitions of fathers and their sons to play for Liverpool often outweighed the element of greed.

Yet I remember one youngster whom we wanted to sign as an

apprentice when he left school. I refused to pay him anything at that time but made him the promise that when he was seventeen and able to sign as a professional we would match, or better, legally in his contract, any other offer made to him. He signed for another First Division club.

This is not the only area of the game where there is corruption. It is not unknown for directors of League clubs who are also on the FA International Committee to abuse their position by 'tapping' another club's player during an England tour. I know for a fact that it happened to one international when he was a Liverpool player.

Unfortunately, this is very difficult to prevent and it happens when players are at their most vulnerable. A budding international who is new to the England scene is unsure both of his position and the power of the man approaching him, so he agrees to talk to avoid jeopardising his new status. Alternatively, the older player approaching the end of his international career is willing to talk because he can see the chance to make a quick buck before he retires.

Tapping generally is an evil the game could well do without, but it is almost impossible to stop because it is rarely done directly. Agents, journalists, friends are all used as middlemen, sometimes unwittingly, and perhaps the only solution might be to introduce a rule that all contracts have to be honoured in full. That might also bring some sanity to the transfer market, which has become ludicrously inflated. A ceiling has got to be introduced, or some clubs are going to perish. UEFA have a ceiling, and so do many continental countries, and I would like to see it established at £400,000.

One of the problems is that so many huge fees are paid on hire-purchase, and while that is all right with lesser amounts it would be wise to rule that anything over, say, £200,000 had to be paid in cash. They have now introduced a system whereby a club can pay 50 per cent down and the rest in instalments over a twelve-month period. That club should be banned from buying another player until the earlier payments have been completed.

I was accused of extravagance when I paid £440,000 for Kenny

Dalglish in 1977, but in actual fact, as I mentioned earlier, I was only using the money we had received from Hamburg for Kevin Keegan – and kept £60,000 change. Even if you subtract the £35,000 we paid Scunthorpe for Kevin, Liverpool were still in the black on the overall deal.

I would have been reluctant to pay a million pounds for a player, particularly in hard cash, but I could have seen myself doing it one way. For instance, if I sold a player for £750,000 and found that the replacement would cost a million, I would add £250,000 to the sum I had received and consider it as a part-exchange deal. I did just that when I bought Mark Lawrenson from Brighton for £900,000 in August 1981, because the sales of Ray Clemence to Spurs and Jimmy Case to Brighton had already provided more than two-thirds of the fee. But paying a million or more for a player places an intolerable financial burden on clubs and adds to the already considerable pressure on managers.

Quite apart from a ceiling, there should also be a formula for establishing a player's value. Ten times his annual wage would make a good starting-point, for it would force clubs to pay their players what they are worth and would eliminate the inflated fee demanded of a richer buyer.

There is no way that a transfer such as that of Mick Robinson from Preston to Manchester City for £750,000 in 1979 should have been allowed to happen. He had only had about a year's Second Division experience, and the fee represented nothing more than pure speculation and a gamble. I would have felt I was taking a risk if I'd paid £150,000 for him! Had we been using a percentage of earnings formula, he would have needed to be earning £75,000 a year at Preston to justify such a fee.

We have certainly come a long way since 1905, when Middlesbrough smashed the transfer record and paid Sunderland for Alf Common the then staggering figure of £1,000.

But the state of the transfer market is only part of the financial structure of the game which needs to be drastically re-designed. Admission prices are another question, because if clubs are going to be paying their top players higher and higher wages and be paying more and more in the transfer market, the money has to come from somewhere. It should not, however, be squeezed from the supporter. The game belongs to the ordinary man in the street, and if it were to price itself out of his reach it would perish.

Yet there are anomalies. Some Third Division clubs charge more for a season ticket than Liverpool, which is ridiculous. On Merseyside, both Liverpool and Everton have always charged about the same, and the basic ground admission price has never been far from the minimum because of the prevailing local conditions of poverty and unemployment. As I said, you relate your prices to what your supporters can afford. We could have probably charged more and got increased revenue from smaller crowds, but that would have had the side effect of reducing the atmosphere in the ground and would very possibly have affected adversely the performances of players. There should, however, be a sliding scale of maximum charges through the divisions to avoid some of the anomalies which exist.

The increase in income which clubs need to compete these days has now got to come from outside the game. Sponsorship is arriving, but archaic rules are preventing its full potential being tapped. Shirt advertising, for example, has got to be allowed, and it is up to the authorities to make sure they do not sign contracts with television companies which contain restrictive clauses.

The fees which television pays at present could also be renegotiated on the principle that if they wish to film the best they should pay the top price. It should be up to clubs to negotiate their own fees, so that, quite fairly, television should have to pay more to cover a championship decider than a throw-away Fourth Division game.

The chairmen, from Hereford to Hartlepool, will disagree and argue that their need is as great as anybody's. The point is, however, that the need is greater at the top if we are to compete on even terms with the best in Europe and the world.

The overheads at a top First Division club are obviously far greater than they are in the Fourth Division, but there is no reason why there should not be a basic amount paid by television into a pool to be shared among the less fortunates of the League. But players' wages have got to be paid, and that represents a lot of money in the First Division. The total wage bill at Anfield has topped a million pounds a year!

People claim that top players are overpaid, but I disagree. They would certainly be well paid if they collected in their wage packets what they were supposed to be earning, but the tax they pay is a crippling factor. They are in the sixty per cent tax bracket and that means that a player earning four times as much as an ordinary bloke on thirty per cent tax in fact picks up only a little more than double.

It is high time more forceful representations were made to the Government to introduce a special tax rate for people with restricted periods of earning. Not many players carry on for more than fifteen years, and the cost of concessions to the Exchequer would be so small as to be insignificant. It would also help in the increasingly difficult fight to keep our best players in this country.

Twenty years ago top players like John Charles, Jimmy Greaves, Denis Law, Joe Baker and Gerry Hitchens were lured to Italy, and it is now happening again. Kevin Keegan and Laurie Cunningham were only the first, followed by Tony Woodcock and Joe Jordan, of what I am sure will be many more football exports.

This is the way the game is going, and it is a trend that I cannot see being reversed. We are no longer playing in our own backyard and we have to acknowledge the threat and competition from overseas and meet the challenge with the competitive spirit on which the game was founded. As international competition increases I am sure we will see more and more of our players leaving and foreign players arriving, but the whole structure and administration of our game must be prepared for it.

So far only a few imported players have been a success, such as Ossie Ardiles, Ricky Villa, Arnold Muhren, Frans Thijssen and one or two others, but a lot have been failures. Maybe it will be a passing trend, as it was at the end of the war when some foreign players were brought in. But at the end of the day everyone likes his own environment, and it requires a lot of character and determination to overcome all the social, climatic and footballing problems associated with competing at top level in a foreign country.

Under the Treaty of Rome it is obviously impossible to limit the number of players from Common Market countries who can play here, but the Government have taken steps to try to safeguard the livelihood of English players threatened with redundancy by the mass cut-backs in staff at a number of clubs, by stricter controls on the issue of work permits.

The Government takes its share of money out of the game without putting much back in the way of grants or incentives, and a little of the encouragement given from that level to some other sports and entertainments would be very welcome in football because, after all, it is our national sport.

But we must earn the right to any help, so the game's administrators have got to get together to provide unity and leadership. They must heed the lessons of others, particularly UEFA, a relatively young body which has approached the problem of developing European football with a sound organisation and an awareness of the demands of the times.

There are lessons to be learned from America, too, where they are gradually becoming organised. They have started from the grassroots by getting interest going in the schools, even if their youngsters cannot yet play the game. They lack the depth of the sport at local level that football has in this country, but it will gradually build up.

There are a lot of obstructions to the development of football in America and they will have problems getting it sufficiently popular so as to compete for support with baseball and their own brand of grid-iron football. A lot of money has been spent by some very wealthy people in trying to establish the game in America, but those people are businessmen, and the hard-nosed American speculator does not throw good dollars after bad, with the result that a lot of clubs have collapsed in the past.

There are lessons to be learned, however, from the way they promote the game although I am not sure that I would like to see American-style razzamatazz in this country. We must be careful, meanwhile, to prevent our own game being weakened by the wholesale transatlantic export of our players by trying to reward our players adequately, so that the dollar is not necessarily greener on the other side.

America is a big country with a massive population, so major sports are not affected unduly by the emergence of others. It is different here, where football is now finding it increasingly hard to combat the growth of other sports and is losing both participants and spectators to them. Cricket, our other national sport, suffered in the same way and had to streamline its administration and competitions. One-day limited-over games, at first shunned by the purists, gave the sport a new lease of life and have even been adopted in the international arena. With floodlights, a white ball, black sight screens and coloured strips, cricket has found a way to compete with the emergent sports, and football must do so too.

This is where the Government, via a permanent all-party agreement, must find ways of helping football, if only by way of tax concessions to players and grants to help the game continue as a major source of entertainment for a large proportion of the citizens of this country.

I always disagreed with the loan system to America, which I am glad was ended, and I never allowed any of my established first-team players to go there in the summer. I believe that the physical and mental demands on top First Division players are such that they need a proper break in the summer – not a busman's holiday. And I also believe that the pre-season period of training and friendly matches is the most vital time of all in preparing players.

The only players I agreed to let go to America were youngsters, who could benefit from the experience, and older players like Tommy Smith and Ian Callaghan, to whom it would have been morally wrong of me to refuse the chance, near the end of their careers, to earn some extra money. Players like them are similar to old cars – they need a run each day, and it is better if they are kept ticking over during the summer. The benefit was seen when they both won European Cup winners' medals after returning from a summer in America.

All in all the next couple of decades are going to be exciting, full of challenge, and could be very rewarding if football in this country responds in the right way. The good things like the FA Cup competition and the strength of our League have got to be preserved. They are fine institutions and the envy of the world.

There have been, and always will be, outcries about the ticket allocation for FA Cup Finals, yet I sympathise with the organisers as they try to fit a pint full of supporters into a half-pint stadium. Until and unless a bigger, more modern stadium than Wembley is constructed, the problems will remain the same and I think the allocation is currently as fair as it can be. When clubs with average gates of more than thirty thousand reach the Cup Final, there will inevitably be disappointed fans, but unlike the Milk Cup Final, the FA Cup Final is a national showpiece. The argument that the county FAs should not get a ticket allocation is wrong, because a place at Wembley is often the sole reward for men who love the game and work dedicatedly at its grassroots without ever being recognised. It is an occasion which belongs to the nation as a whole, not just to the competing clubs, and when it is being beamed by satellite into the living-rooms of the world, it is something of which we can be justifiably proud.

That is more than can be said for the hooligans and vandals who infest the terraces. I cannot come up with the ideal solution, for I do believe that if soccer ceased to exist they would just find somewhere else to cause trouble. They are the products of a society in which discipline and respect for authority have been superseded by selfishness and rebelliousness, and they would wantonly wreck a flower show if there were no other available target. They are one of the bad elements of the game which have got to be weeded out and destroyed before they kill from within. The sooner this happens, the better.

My only regret is that I shall not be part of it, because I have always thrived on challenge.

9 Mind and Body

It's not very pleasant to pick up a newspaper and read that you're unpatriotic, especially when you've served your country in a war. But that's virtually what happened to me over England's refusal of an invitation to take part in a tournament in Uruguay.

The idea was for all past World Cup winners to compete against each other during two weeks right in the middle of the 1980–81 season. The Press in particular seemed to think it would be a national disgrace if we didn't go. But there wasn't much support for the idea when representatives of four clubs – Manchester United, Nottingham Forest, Crystal Palace and Liverpool – were called together for a meeting in Manchester to discuss the matter with the FA and the Football League. Nottingham Forest didn't even turn up!

It was suggested that we would be the four clubs who would provide all the players and that our League programmes would be suspended for the few weeks while our men were away in South America.

My main objection to it was that we didn't really know what effect the change of climate, the eighteen-hour flight and the time difference would have on the players, not just for the time they were away, but for some time afterwards as well. Many people do not fully appreciate the different effects that going into a plane can have on different individuals. I have known players and journalists, indeed people in all walks of life, who are frightened to death of flying and whose whole system can be upset by it.

My concern was for my club, Liverpool. I simply stated that while it might seem to some people that a couple of weeks away could do no harm, I was worried that the effects might carry over for weeks afterwards.

We are proud of our reputation for consistency at Anfield, and our consistency is not bred from nothing. There is a great deal of thought behind it. This was a classic case of people jumping on the bandwagon without giving any thought to the way it could affect athletes. Those who shouted loudest for England's participation were not those who would have to go to South America and perform – and maybe carry the after-effects into their League performances for weeks after their return.

Ron Greenwood, then England manager, was at that meeting in Manchester, and I'm sure he agreed with many of the things I said. A few weeks later, he sent Ray Clemence back from an England game with a copy of *FIFA News* opened at an article headed 'Air Travel Fatigue in Football Players'.

In the article Professor Dr Jean Vittori, of the FIFA medical committee, discussed the problems of fatigue on passengers, saying that 'air travel constitutes a heavy physiological assault on man'. He went on to discuss in detail the effects of flying at a very high altitude in a pressurised cabin, the enormous trouble from the rapid change in climatic conditions, and the disturbance of the body rhythms due to time changes and the effects of noise and vibration. He concluded that the fear of accidents suffered by many passengers is an additional cause of fatigue that cannot be overlooked.

We had first-hand experience of the kind of fatigue the professor refers to when we lost 3–0 to Flamengo of Brazil in the World Club Championship in Tokyo in December 1981. We met Arsenal at Anfield on the Tuesday night in a League Cup replay, and left for Tokyo the following morning. Because of the weather in England, we had to go on icy roads to Manchester and then on to London. In all it took almost twenty-four hours to get to Japan.

We certainly needed more time for acclimatisation before playing the match on the Sunday. The body rhythms were upset then – and I'm sure we were still suffering the after-effects a fortnight after getting back to England.

Manchester City beat us at Anfield in our first match after our return, and I knew that I for one still wasn't right. Apart from the physical effects, I didn't feel as sharp in my mind as normal. It must have affected the players too. It goes against everything you preach when you are trying to get players fit.

I've referred to the effects of air travel because it shows how we have moved on since I was a player, but this progress had brought problems of mind and body which can never be underestimated.

The body has been a particular interest of mine through most of my time in football. In fact, without that interest I doubt whether I would be where I am today. I might have returned to bricklaying after finishing as a player. As it was, I stayed in the game, first as a trainer, then as assistant manager, and later as manager of Liverpool.

I doubt whether I would have got very far without some help right at the start from Sir John Moores, a man associated with Everton rather than Liverpool. Some people on Merseyside today may look at me and say that Sir John has a lot to answer for.

I was always interested in physiotherapy when I was a player. I took a correspondence course for two years before I hung my boots up. Then Sir John fixed me up with a full-time course. It meant going to Belmont Road Hospital from nine to five every day. The late Norman Borrowdale, who treated the Everton players, was a physiotherapist at the hospital.

It was all changing then from what it had been through most of my playing days. Then it was the hot and cold water treatment. Trainers had to have hands like leather. There was hardly a player who got by without suffering first-degree burns at some time or other. You put the hot towel on and then the cold one, it was the main treatment.

It never really did any harm, just as the cold sponge does no harm – even if it often does no good either. Some of the sprays used today can be harmful to skin tissue if they are used without expert knowledge.

The first person I ever treated was Albert Shelley, our first-team trainer, for a boil on the backside. Albert was one of the old school. He taught me how to harden my hands with the towels. When the physio machines came in I had to show him how to use them, but he never really came to terms with them. He had a common-sense approach to the practical side of it, but he was frightened by the electrical stuff – he even used to put a handkerchief on the leads. So when the machines came I virtually took over the treatment of all the players.

Through the years my experience taught me to spot an injury very early. Sometimes I've spotted things, even from television, and made an instant diagnosis. Others have disagreed, but many times I've been proved right eventually.

I remember seeing Ian Callaghan go down with a bent knee and hurt himself during pre-season training one year. I saw something from the way he fell. Bill Shankly was in hospital at the time, and when I went to visit him I told him I thought Cally had done a cartilage. Bill didn't want to believe it. When Bill came out of hospital, Cally said it was his ankle that was sore. Bill said he knew it. Cally played a few games for us at the start of the season, then he had to have a cartilage operation.

Colin Bell was one player I saw injured while I was watching television. It was against Manchester United in the League Cup. I said it was a bad one straight away, and unfortunately Colin, who had been a great player for Manchester City and England, was never the same again. After a long hard struggle to get back, he finally had to retire, because of that injury.

Charlie George played against us for Derby County at Anfield one week. He was injured and had to come off. Tommy Docherty said Charlie might have been pulling the wool over his eyes because we had just gone 3–0 ahead. I said I would have to look at the incident again on television before I made up my mind.

Charlie just seemed to touch Ray Kennedy in the air and when he came down he landed straight-legged and crumpled up. I knew there was something wrong. At least three or four months later, Southampton bought him for £400,000, but he hardly played a game for them before the end of the season. When Liverpool played Southampton down at the Dell, I told Lawrie McMenemy that I still thought George had damaged a cartilage. Lawrie thought it impossible because his muscle had built up so well. About a fortnight later he had to have an operation. Cartilage.

I went to watch Derby play Orient one day, and David Nish

went down as they were kicking in before the game. Having had two cartilages out since I finished playing, I knew what it was. I told our lads when I got back and when I saw Dave Mackay, the Derby manager, I told him as well. They didn't agree with me at Derby, but again I was right.

Although I've often spotted injuries quickly, we've not always acted on them ourselves. In the first game of the 1966–67 season against Leicester, Gerry Byrne wrenched everything when he stubbed his foot in the turf. I knew what was wrong, but for some reason or other we delayed the operation.

Gerry Byrne was an incredibly hard man. Nobody who saw him in the FA Cup Final against Leeds in 1965 can doubt that. He was injured in an incident with Bobby Collins after only nine minutes, and I went on to treat him because he had taken the skin off his shin. He didn't mention anything else. Then, when a Leeds player was injured a little later on, I took the opportunity to go on and see Gerry again.

I felt his collarbone and could tell straight away that it was broken. There were no substitutes in those days. I told him that if I were in his place I would have to have a wooden leg before I went off. I then went back to Bill and, very quietly, as Don Revie was sitting on the bench nearby and I was frightened he might overhear, told him that Gerry had broken his collarbone.

At half-time I put a figure-of-eight bandage on Gerry, and he went out again and did tremendously well. The game went into extra time and there were only a few of us in the 100,000 crowd who knew the agony Gerry was in. Leeds had no idea at all. Gerry even went through and laid on the cross for Roger Hunt to get our first goal. At the end I sent for the Wembley doctor, who said there was no way it was broken. But I insisted that Gerry had an X-ray, and, sure enough, it was.

The following season, Gerry dislocated his elbow in the European Cup Winners' Cup match against Celtic at Parkhead. He was in great pain, but our club doctor, Jack Reid, did a tremendous job on it and he stayed on until ten minutes from the end. I took him to hospital the next day, his arm was black from the wrist to the shoulder, but there was no break. The next day he played in our League match against Stoke City!

We've been lucky in a way at Liverpool. We've had our share of hardy customers, men like Gerry Byrne who could play even when they were injured. Tommy Smith and Emlyn Hughes are two obvious examples, but Chris Lawler, although possibly not so obvious to the public, was probably the finest example of all.

When he had that run of 315 consecutive first-team appearances, it wasn't just a question of luck in avoiding injuries. He had his share of injuries, but often he played where lesser men would have cried off. But, there again, he didn't fling himself around and take risks like other players. He didn't rely on physical speed, his speed was in his head. Nobody would notice when he was injured.

Emlyn might even have been helped into settling into his centre-back position by playing on with an injury. He had been a bit of a tearaway in midfield, and if he had a weakness when he switched to the back it was that he made too many sorties upfield. Then he had a torn knee ligament, but he played on with it and that season we went on to win the FA Cup. That injury helped to bring more discipline into his play. Many players wouldn't have been able to play with such an injury, but he did.

Tommy was another one. He carried an injury for a long time. He had what we call a 'Baker's cyst' in the back of the knee. In the end we had to take him to see a specialist, and he decided to operate. Even then Tommy thought he would be back in action in a couple of days, when in fact it was a nine-week job.

He may have been lucky that with his reputation, opposing players often tended to keep away from him on the field. He seldom got exposed, even when carrying an injury. Against certain sides, we knew he could have gone out and done his stuff on one leg.

To a lesser extent, reputation probably came into it with Emlyn, too. He had that 'Crazy Horse' tag. He was never the same in his tackling as Tommy, but he was an awkward customer to tangle with, as he seemed at times to be all arms and legs. He also had that special brand of Liverpool determination.

The mind plays a big part in all this. Not only the mind of the individual concerned, but the mind of the person he is playing against. I'm sure that Tommy often went out there as the most confident man on the park, even though he was only half fit, because he knew the opposition that day wouldn't expose him. Norman Hunter must have operated on the same principle at times, revelling in the hard man image, and knowing that the opponent was losing sleep at the prospect of facing him the next day. Mind you, they could sometimes be unsettled themselves by a young upstart who wasn't bothered about reputations.

Players have to be aware of the mental approach to the game all the time. You look out to see how your opponent reacts, particularly before a match. Kevin Lewis, our winger when we came up from the Second Division, looked as if he didn't have a care in the world. But he was so highly strung that he was sick before he went out on the field. Alan Hansen is another one, looking cool, calm and collected. But when it's all over he'll admit he was a bag of nerves beforehand.

You have to take factors like this into account, especially in getting players fit, and particularly now that they are under more pressure than players have ever been. You don't know if a fellow has a problem at home or what he's got on his mind. But you have to sift it out, otherwise there is no way he can give his best. Experience tells you when there's something wrong, mentally as well as physically.

Soon after I took over I had an idea that I felt could eradicate one of the few weaknesses in Ray Clemence. Very few people noticed it, but it worked. At Anfield on match days, we used to fly flags from the top of the Kemlyn Road stand. The players running out on to the pitch from the main stand had a good view of these flags. In particular, they could tell when it was windy.

When there is a wind, Anfield is one of the trickiest grounds in the country, and it showed in the flags, particularly when the wind was blowing from the Kop end. Ray hated the wind. His biggest problem was his deadball kicking, and it was worse when he tried to kick into the wind. If he worried about his kicking, it could also affect other parts of his game.

I decided it was no good letting him worry about how bad the wind was by letting him see the way those flags were blowing as he came out of the tunnel. The flags went, and Ray's kicking improved. I'm sure he felt easier in himself because he wasn't constantly being reminded that there was a wind blowing.

Some say we're lucky at Liverpool because we have fewer injuries than almost any other club. I certainly wouldn't deny that luck comes in it. You need some luck to set the record achieved in our championship season of 1965–66 of using only fourteen players – of whom Bobby Graham made only one appearance and Alf Arrowsmith a mere three. When we set the First Division points records of sixty-eight in 1978–79 we used only fifteen players altogether. But there's much more to it than just luck. There's the factor of competition, which makes players unwilling to drop out because they're worried about getting back in, particularly when the team is winning. It is noticeable that teams having a bad time seem to get hit with more injuries. I think the way we prepare and train also has a lot to do with it.

There are five things generally accepted to be necessary to make a footballer: *skill*, *strength*, *stamina*, *speed* and *flexibility*. You have to bear these factors in mind when you are putting your training programme together.

The whole scene is a *stamina* test, a marathon race. *Strength* has to be developed from the start. You build that up, giving the player a higher resistance to things. *Skill* comes next, developed with a constant repetition of pattern. *Speed* comes after you've run them in. Then you start to get them stretching out. *Flexibility* is important, and we probably suffer in this country because of our climate. It's a well-known fact that players performing in warmer climates have a wider range of movements.

Some say that flexibility exercises are 'pansified' – they are certainly much maligned. But if you're not tuned in properly you can do yourself a mischief, perhaps even suffer a serious injury that could put you out of the game for a season or even longer.

How you go about it can have a lot to do with how players withstand injuries. I always think it's like running a car in – you take it easy at first. Then, when you feel it's ready, you open it up. It's the same with people. It's so easy to over-train, and you have to be tuned in to make sure this doesn't happen. When the usual glut of fixtures comes along, you have to be able to recognise that there still has to be a relaxation period, irrespective of performances.

This is often done when you are having a bad time. You might have had a bad result and you pick up the paper and read that you should lambast the players and give them a heavy session. But relaxation is a big part of the training programme, and as important as doing your exercises properly. Sometimes you have to allow them to relax, even if to others at the time it doesn't seem the right thing to do. It's not always easy to make the decision to let the players relax, but there can be a benefit later on.

As I have said, the preparation is very important, and the way we have prepared has helped us at times to avoid injuries. But there was a time, when, without realising it, we didn't prepare the team properly for a new season.

It was in the summer of 1970, when the main stand at Anfield was being rebuilt. Previously we had always reported to Anfield in the morning, stripped there and then gone in the bus to Melwood, our training ground. Then, we'd go back in the bus to Anfield, change, and have our lunch. But at this time the lads reported straight to Melwood and afterwards to the Mons Hotel in Bootle for lunch.

Many players went straight from the training session into the bath, put their clothes on and dived off for lunch. And in the next few months we had just about the worst spate of injuries since I'd been at the club. First, Ian Callaghan had to have a cartilage operation, then Bobby Graham broke his ankle. Later, Peter Thompson and Alun Evans had to have cartilage operations too. These were all regular first-team players at the time. We also had a couple of the apprentices needing cartilage operations.

I discussed it with Bill, who was a fitness fanatic and also knew a bit about the medical side. I pointed out the benefit of the normal routine. That is when players come off the training field, sit down while they have a cup of tea, and then relax on the bus back to Anfield before having their bath and changing. It was what I called the warming-down period – and it is as important as warming up at the start of a training session. We soon went back to the old routine, and it's the same routine that Liverpool use today.

Football is a game that involves intense muscular strain, frequent bodily contact, and constant changes of direction and pace. The climate and state of the pitch can affect all this and can produce a crop of injuries. Conditions are something that you have to be fully aware of in the build-up. It is essential that before the players go out they go through a good warm-up session, and afterwards a warming-down period as well.

So while the main stand was being built the players didn't get the proper warming-down period, and we had all those injuries. Fatigue was left in their systems. It was still there when the players were performing in the games early that season. Even when we had what appeared to be accidental injuries, I still wondered whether it was a throwback to that change of routine.

It's stating the obvious that early diagnosis is important in the treatment of football injuries. There are cases of players whose careers could have been seriously affected because the correct diagnosis was not made early on in their careers.

I think of players like Eddie Gray of Leeds, and John Toshack at Liverpool. I don't know that much about Eddie, but I would think he suffered in a similar way to Tosh – probably because in their youthful eagerness they played when they had not made a proper recovery from an injury. I've no doubt, from the way Tosh's injury developed while he was with Liverpool, that it was an early injury at Cardiff that caused his chronic condition. It's no crime, it's no criticism of anybody, but it does show what you have to guard against from the earliest moments of a player's career.

There are many times when players don't like you telling them there's something wrong with them. They think you just want to get them out of the team. There were some awkward moments with Tosh.

Tosh's injury was in the thigh. He had pulled a muscle and then aggravated the injury, and it caused calcification. At the moment, there's no cure for it. It has to be nursed along, and the player has to be prepared to go through the pain barrier.

It all goes back to taking precautions early on. It didn't matter how small an injury might be, at Liverpool we hauled the player in for treatment. We didn't make a song and dance about it, but we made sure the player was treated.

I've heard that Eddie, like Tosh, had an injury early in his career and was so keen to play that he did so before he was fully recovered. These are only two cases I've heard of, there must be hundreds of others.

While this can be a problem at our level, with clubs that have good squads, you can imagine how much more of a problem it can be when you don't have such a good squad. An injured player can be pushed too hard when he should be resting and recovering. That's one of the obvious advantages of a big squad, they are needed more than ever today with the number of games you have to play in a season.

I've written about the players we've had who have carried on even when they've had injuries. But none of them would ever have been allowed to play on if we had felt there was a risk of permanent damage. There's no way we would dice with muscle or internal injuries. But there are injuries you can protect, so that the player can carry on without anyone ever noticing, as Chris Lawler did so often.

Diet, of course, is important to any athlete. We are probably able to watch a footballer's diet more than we used to. We have the players more in our sights now. We know what they eat - and often we can govern what they eat.

We watch their weight, frequently putting them on the scales, because with all the travelling we do, excess weight can easily be gained. When people are away from home they often tend to pick at things, eating for eating's sake. And travelling abroad we have to watch what is served up to us in the meals we have ordered. It would be so easy to upset the result of a game by eating something that wasn't right for you. You have to be ultra careful.

Of course the drinking has to be watched too. You have to give the players a certain amount of licence, but you also have to let them know if it goes too far. Self-discipline comes into this too. One knows that the clowns can get carried away in company, but the sensible ones can sit there looking after themselves.

There are times when players should be allowed to let their hair down. Some people say that it shouldn't be in the season, that they have their summer break for that. But there is more pressure on players now, particularly at the level our lads compete, than there ever has been. We were knocked out of the European Cup by Nottingham Forest when we thought we might go on and win it for the third time. Naturally I was upset and disappointed. At times like that you might think to yourself that you should tighten up, but then you realise that the players have been turned over mentally, so you have to be careful. That could be just the time when they need to let their hair down a bit.

Mind and body, the mental and physical processes, are closely linked, and it would be dangerous to ignore that fact.

The horse that grins and bears me! My second love is horses. I spend a lot of my time at Frankie Durr's stables. This was taken at Frankie Carr's.

A charity dinner in Liverpool – all part of a manager's life.

The fans who make it all worthwhile.

Success again with the UEFA Cup, Charity Shield and Championship Trophy.

Receiving my Bell's Manager of the Month Award at Anfield in January 1983 – for a record 20th time. The tally so far is: Manager of the Month, 11 awards; Manager of the Year, 5 awards; Divisional Manager of the Month, 2 awards; Special awards, 2.

Keeping fit – I am still the best on this ball in Liverpool FC.

Who said we never talked together! With Gordon Lee, then manager of Everton, in no-man's-land, Stanley Park.

Yet another award – this time from the *Evening Standard* in London.

ABOVE A quiet game of cricket at Oxton.

LEFT A nice cup of tea with my wife Jessie.

Four birthday cakes and forty-three candles to celebrate my forty-three years at Anfield, 8 May 1982.

With my brother Hughie, some Helton schoolchildren and the European Cup.

The team behind the team in 1980. *Left to right:* Roy Evans, Tommy Smith, Ronnie Moran, Eli Wass, Tom Saunders, Reuben Bennett, John Bennison, Geoff Twentyman, Joe Fagan, Arthur Riley and me.

Time to reflect.

Time to hand over the reins.

10 Referees

A referee's lot is not a happy one. He has to take abuse from managers, players and supporters; his decisions, made on the spot, are examined by television with the aid of slow-motion replays; he has a spy in the stand checking his performance; and he is generally the butt for everyone. I would certainly not do the job for the money they get.

I have no doubt that referees are basically honest and do the job because they love the involvement with the game. It's not an easy job, and I believe they do their best. However, I am sure that the standard of refereeing could be improved, and it is the responsibility of everyone connected with football to strive constantly to improve it.

Many people advocate professional referees, but I have reservations about that because if they mingled with the professional players at clubs there would be a risk of them becoming too familiar – and we all know that familiarity breeds contempt. I feel that the amateur referee has a greater sense of authority and objectivity because it is only when he's in charge of a match that he has involvement with the game as a whole.

He earns his living away from football, but the problem there is that an amateur can hide from criticism behind the excuse that he only does the job for the love of the game, whereas a professional would have to think a lot more deeply about his performance.

You can argue it both ways and not come up with a clear case either for or against professional referees, but I think, for the moment at any rate, that football cannot afford them. There are almost a hundred referees on the Football League list, so if you paid them roughly what players get it would cost in the region of £1,500,000 a year.

It has been suggested that a referee should be attached to each club so that he can train with and get to know and understand the professional player and appreciate the machinations of the game. But I cannot see the bread-line clubs of the Fourth Division, in particular, being able to afford an extra name on their payroll, because, after all, it's only a handful of the top clubs who are in the black. The game owes millions of pounds in bank overdrafts, and the aim must first be to reduce them and put football back on a more stable financial footing rather than to worsen the position.

I think it is more realistic to approach the problem of improving referee's performances by trying to pin-point and eliminate some of their problems.

One of the basic troubles is fitness, and I don't mean just the ability to run up and down a pitch for ninety minutes. Mental fitness is just as important, because anticipation – and I do not mean pre-judgement – comes from the alertness of the mind and helps a referee keep up with the play and also find better positions from which to make decisions.

One reason why I always refrain from comparing referees from my playing days with present day officials is the change in the pattern of play. When the likes of Tom Finney and Sir Stanley Matthews were jinking about with the ball it was easier for the referee to keep up with the play because it all centred around the ball. He could have a breather at times, because the game was far more individual, players held the ball for longer.

The emphasis has shifted these days and it is what a player does *off* the ball which is important, so the referee has had to widen his field of vision in order to pick up off-the-ball movements of players, so that he can anticipate a quick break.

The tendency now is for teams to contain the opposition and then strike forward quickly when the opportunity arises. This is where the anticipation comes in. A good referee will be alert to this tactic and therefore be able to keep up with the play when the break occurs. A poor referee will be caught out and left behind. He knows it, and blows up at the first sign of an infringement so that he can catch up again, even if it is at the expense of the advantage rule. And that can land the referee in even more trouble, because such action leads to frustration among the players and the crowd, making the rest of the match even harder to control.

Thus mental fitness is as important to a referee as it is to a player, and to help him achieve it, he must have the right preparation for a game. A long drive to a match and a heavy, stodgy meal in a motorway service area, which is the enforced routine of some referees, is no way to prepare, because the effect is tiredness and sluggishness.

The League tried to overcome the problem and reduce the costs in expenses by sparing northern-based referees matches in the south and vice-versa. Yet some officials still have journeys of three or four hours, particularly when conditions are bad in the middle of winter. I think a referee should spend the night before a match in an hotel if his journey is more than fifty miles.

That attempt by the League also had the side-effect of sometimes putting an extra burden on the shoulders of an official. For instance, a referee from one of the home counties controlling a match in London between a southern and a northern team could have the subconscious fear of being labelled a 'homer', and biased, if he had to give the majority of the decisions for the home side. And that fear can quite easily have the reverse effect of him handicapping that side by refusing to give decisions for them in a misguided attempt to prove his impartiality.

Referees are only human and, like the rest of us, all have different personalities. I know at Anfield that the reputation of the Kop has varying affects on referees. Some will be intimidated and give a majority of the fifty-fifty decisions in Liverpool's favour, while others will take a defiant stance and, in effect, tell the Kop to go to hell by giving those fifty-fifty decisions the other way.

This is one area where something should be done, and the same goes for those referees who inadvertently handicap the better sides. Some have a tendency when a top side is playing a team from the bottom of the table not to penalise as many of the inferior team's offences as they should. The attitude is: Well, they're a good side anyway – they'll win in the end. Again the frustration element creeps in.

Another problem is referees who get a bee in their bonnet about something. They pick out a certain law, go looking for an infringement of it and then apply it to the letter, while at the same time ignoring other offences. We had a referee once at Highbury whose particular fad was the goalkeeper's four-step rule. That referee's interpretation, unlike that of almost all the others, was to count the steps taken by a goalkeeper even while the ball was rolling along the ground and he wasn't actually holding it. Ray Clemence, and every other goalkeeper I can think of, had been doing it for years, and Ray was baffled when he was penalised. He didn't know what he had done wrong. Later this rule was sensibly clarified.

Clive Thomas used always to be on the look-out for goalkeepers lifting their feet, but it is an area where a lot of discretion has to be used. There is a world of difference between deliberately raising a foot to an opponent and the natural result of jumping. Phil Parkes, Dai Davies and Ray Clemence were all in trouble with Clive Thomas because of that – three highly respected international goalkeepers.

They are fads which some referees have, and they usually represent a flaw. It is certainly a problem and one which must be solved if there is going to be any consistency in the application of the rules.

Clive Thomas had another flaw earlier in his career, when he was known as 'Thomas the Book'. The League issued instructions to referees to be stricter with players infringing the rules, and to caution them, particularly for tackles from behind, dissent and deliberate hand-ball.

Basically, the instruction was a good one, but Thomas carried it to absurd lengths, and after one match I went to him to query why a certain player had been booked. He went to take his book out, and I said, 'You might as well take my name – you've taken everyone else's.'

Obviously there are occasions when referees have no option but to caution players, but often it is unnecessary, and spoils the flow of the game. A player who has been booked becomes frightened of being sent off if he commits another, often trivial, offence, and as a result his effectiveness to his team is lost. There is also the halt in play with the crowd often wondering what has happened.

Fortunately, Clive Thomas learned his lesson, used his discretion more, and as a result became a better, though no less authoritative, referee. Since then referees have had instructions to be more stringent than ever, and Clive and his colleagues have had to come to terms with that.

Some of them think they have to be conspicuous, and Roger Kirkpatrick, 'Mr Pickwick' as he was known, with his high-stepping, sprinting style, was one of them. Whether some referees set out to get themselves noticed for the benefit of the assessor in the stand, or whether they are on an ego-trip, thinking *they* must put on a show for the public because they are on the pitch too, I don't know. But it is particularly noticeable when well-known referees take charge of matches in the Third or Fourth Divisions.

Perhaps it is because their mental attitude is not quite right, rather like a First Division side playing a non-League side in the Cup, because they find the atmosphere in the Fourth Division doesn't provide the motivation and concentration produced at top level, but they don't officiate as efficiently. Yet, it should not happen, because the rules are the same, and any team, no matter which, is entitled to the same treatment as a First Division side.

A man who was a perfect example to referees was Arthur Ellis. He controlled a number of games in which I played, and I had the greatest respect for him, possibly stemming from an incident in a game against Middlesbrough. I was playing against Lindy Delapenha and when he beat me on one occasion I said to him, 'Do that again and I'll part your hair.'

It was a deliberate attempt on my part to frighten him and, if I had done it today in the hearing of the referee, I have no doubt I would be booked for ungentlemanly conduct. Arthur Ellis heard me, and he let play continue. He didn't interrupt the flow and deprive Middlesbrough of the advantage Delapenha had given them. Instead, a couple of minutes later, I found him running beside me – and offering me a comb. 'Do you want to borrow this?' he said. It put me in my place and I didn't need another warning. I would like to see more referees using a bit of subtlety in awkward moments.

It was a perfect example of a referee using common sense, because there are more ways of putting someone down than by booking them. Of course there are times when a referee has no alternative but to caution a player, and those occasions are usually obvious to the crowd.

Sometimes, however, the crowd is baffled, and becomes frustrated and angry, and the continuity of the game is broken by the hold-up. Such situations get the referee into worse trouble than if he had used his common sense, and taken no action other than to have a quiet word with the player concerned while the game was carrying on.

The introduction of the yellow and red cards caused a number of unforeseen problems. It was at times when the play was stopped and a player shown a card for an incident which the crowd hadn't seen that trouble arose. The abolition, in domestic matches, of the card, with the referee reverting back to the old booking system was, I think, a good one because it let the referee off the hook.

If he has a card in his pocket it is only too easy to produce it, instantly, without a second thought. When that system was abolished in this country it gave the official two or three yards in which to have second thoughts, and that extra thinking time gave him greater scope for discretion. When the cards were being used, I am sure that a number of referees would have had second thoughts if they had had more time to weigh up the situation and would have loved to have been able to put the card back – but by then it was too late.

A classic example was our European Cup quarter-final defeat in Sofia when Mark Lawrenson was sent off. One of the CSKA players, Yonchev, did something and Mark threatened to retaliate. The linesman, who was right by the incident, raised his flag and the referee, who was fully twenty-five yards away, pulled out the red card as he ran to the scene. It was tough on Mark to become the first player we had sent off in eighteen years in Europe, and a three-match ban was particularly harsh because he insisted, and I believe him, that he never touched Yonchev, who aggravated the incident by collapsing to the ground.

Had the card system not been in use, I'm sure Mark would not have been sent off because the referee would have had the time, while he was making his way to the scene, to make a fuller assessment of the situation - and, perhaps, it was fortunate for the ref that the incident happened in Sofia, and not at Anfield, because of the possible reaction of the spectators.

Mervyn Griffiths was another referee in my playing days for whom I had a lot of respect - even if he did disallow a goal from Billy Liddell against Manchester City which cost us our place in the Cup because he'd already blown for full time.

One official I felt I would have had good reason to take to task was Pat Partridge, but I would probably have been hauled over the coals for bringing the game into disrepute if I had said everything I felt. Like me, Pat is from the North-East, and as a northern-based official he quite often refereed Liverpool games.

But two games in particular remain very sore memories. They were the League Cup Final and the replay against Nottingham Forest in 1978. It was the only domestic trophy Liverpool had never won - not that that had anything to do with it - but I am convinced we were not only the better team but that we should have won the Cup.

I'm not taking anything away from Forest or their young goalkeeper, Chris Woods, who played in place of the Cup-tied Peter Shilton and performed magnificently in both games. But after outplaying Forest at Wembley we had a perfectly good goal by Terry McDermott disallowed for offside because of Pat Partridge's interpretation of the rule relating to 'interference with play'.

Everybody in the stadium, Forest players included, accepted that it was a good goal when Terry fired in, but Pat Partridge thought otherwise and ruled Kenny Dalglish offside. Add to that the blatant penalty offence when Dalglish was tripped by Kenny Burns with the route to goal wide open, and you can begin to understand my sense of injustice. Yet that was nothing compared with the way Pat Partridge handled the replay at Old Trafford.

There were three incidents in that game in which I am certain he made wrong decisions. The first was the penalty he awarded to Forest after Phil Thompson had committed a professional foul on John O'Hare when he had a good scoring chance. You can claim that it was poetic justice because the professional foul is morally wrong, and the authorities have since tried to eradicate it by sending off the offender.

Pat Partridge had been in the game long enough to know that Phil had a choice between the devil and the deep blue sea. He could either let O'Hare go, risking a goal and a tongue-lashing from me, or commit the foul and accept the inevitable booking.

But what Phil would not do, and did not do, was bring O'Hare down in the penalty area, because that would have increased considerably the risk of a goal. Phil committed the foul a yard outside the penalty area, as the television cameras at the game proved – and that is not a penalty, no matter how much anyone claims it was poetic justice.

The referee obviously had it in his mind that it was such a blatant foul that it deserved the punishment of a penalty. But he is there to control the game according to the rules of the game, and it has never been in the rules that a penalty *can* be awarded for a foul anywhere on the pitch – only inside the penalty area. If he was in doubt of the actual place of the foul, he should have consulted a linesman, and if he thought the offence to be so bad, he should have sent Phil off – as would happen now under the stricter code.

Pat Partridge put his own head in a noose when he admitted afterwards that he was ten yards behind play but was convinced it was a penalty. I have already given my views on referees keeping up with play. He was caught again a few minutes later when we broke quickly, and the ball was played forward to Terry McDermott, who controlled it with the top left-hand side of his chest and went on to put the ball in the net for what would have been the equaliser.

The referee was in no position to judge whether Terry's arm played any part in controlling the ball, and he had to rely on a linesman's decision. Even in those intimate moments of confession Terry has sworn that it didn't touch his arm. But, be that as it may, the referee should have been in the right position to make a decision of his own.

To rub salt in our wounds Pat Partridge also found it necessary to book Ian Callaghan for the first time in 849 games for Liverpool for what was a perfectly legitimate shoulder charge on Peter Withe. Even the Forest striker himself told the referee that the challenge was fair!

The Phil Thompson incident also had an unfortunate side-effect, directly attributable to the referee's mistake. Because it was the controversial and decisive moment in the game, it was naturally highlighted on television, whereas it might not have been if the correct decision of a direct free-kick outside the box had been given. As a result, Phil was hustled in front of microphones when mentally he was in no condition to comment, and admitted publicly that he had committed a professional foul. That admission had him hauled before the FA for bringing the game into disrepute. Altogether we felt they were two most unsatisfactory refereeing performances by Pat Partridge.

Fitness and uniformity of interpretation are only two of the ways I think the standard of refereeing can be improved. Another way would be to appoint for an entire season a referee and two linesmen to work as a team. In that way, you would eliminate the misunderstandings which sometimes occur between officials who have never met and certainly never controlled a game together before. This is not dissimilar to the system used by UEFA, whose matches are always controlled by three officials from the same country. I have noticed that in European games linesmen don't dither in flagging for a refereeing decision and I think in some respects European referees are better than ours.

It comes back to my point about keeping up with the play when a team breaks quickly. They have been playing that system on the Continent much longer than we have, and referees are more alive to the dangers of being left behind by the play. Perhaps, too, the large oval stadiums that are commonplace in Europe have something to do with it, because without the crowd breathing down his neck the referee feels under less pressure.

But I would like to see officials working as teams, and they could have a table of their own based on the marks of the assessor. They could even have their own system of promotion and relegation which would allow the promising youngsters to come through more quickly than at present, and the older, more experienced, yet less efficient ones to be gradually phased out. It would assist in the appointment of the top men for the top jobs at important or difficult matches such as promotion or relegation battles, derby matches, Cup Finals and the like. If such a system was adopted there would be a howl of protest from the lower divisions that they would be getting second-best, but in my experience, as I have said, the top names do not perform so efficiently in the lower divisions.

Football is a team game and it would do no harm for the officials to work as a team as well. I'm sure it would improve the standard of control. The system might prove a bit boring to the linesmen, but while they might have to wait a little longer before their promotion to the middle, they would benefit by having any repeated mistakes corrected by the referee in charge of the team, whose familiarity with his linesmen would allow him to spot them.

There was an example of inconsistency during our Boxing Day game with Manchester United in 1979, when the linesmen were giving different interpretations of the off-side law. One was flagging for everything, while the other was letting play continue if the player in an off-side position was not interfering with play.

Had the three officials been working as a team, that sort of inconsistency would have been eliminated, and they could have explained their interpretation of that and other laws to the two sides before the match. If I had been the assessor at the match it would have been the first thing I mentioned in my report, and assessors could help considerably in the development of a referee and his linesmen as a team. Any inconsistency which occurred regularly, like the one I have mentioned, would be pointed out to the three officials, and as a result their performance would be improved. A greater level of consistency would be to everyone's benefit. Deliberate handball was a case in point. Before the professional foul edict it was a bookable offence, and while most referees booked a player for it outside the penalty area, some didn't when a player prevented a goal by using his hands. It's as if the referee felt a penalty was sufficient punishment - yet the offence is the same wherever it's committed.

There are a number of things which happen behind the scenes which I am far from happy about. I've heard well-known referees say they should be made to feel part of the clubs they visit, and that the welcome mat should be rolled out. But here again I feel the best referees are those whom you are hardly aware of. I like to see a referee arrive at the ground, have a cup of tea, go out and do his job, and then leave with the minimum amount of socialising.

In the old days, there was not as much socialising by referees, but there have been several factors behind its increase. The growth of the world game, and in particular the World Cup, has elevated some top referees into internationally known figures, and television, by highlighting decisions, have made others household names. They are now asked to make personal appearances, open this and that and make speeches, all of which was almost unknown thirty years ago, and which has boosted the egos of all but the most level-headed.

It has made it more difficult for them and the new familiarity also makes it harder for managers and players. You get linesmen coming into the dressing-rooms with autograph books and looking for favours, and although it might sound silly, it does put you in a difficult position. It is an obstacle, but it does not become apparent until you see the reaction to the familiarity out on the pitch. As I say, it is far better if people do not know they are there.

Another danger is if a player is on christian name terms with a referee. Emlyn Hughes was once severely reprimanded for saying 'Hello Keith' when Keith Walker entered our dressing-room before a match. They had known each other since Emlyn's Blackpool days when they trained together on the beach.

I knew that Emlyn, a bubbling extrovert character, was only being friendly, but referees and players have got to have mutual respect and if you start using christian names with referees before a match you can have problems on the field. The official is aware of the dangers of favouring a player because of a friendship, and sometimes even over-compensates for it by booking him for a remark which might be all right between friends in a pub, but not between a referee and a player on a football pitch.

As I've said before, a referee's job is not an easy one, and it was not helped by the orders they were given to go to the dressing-rooms before matches to check studs. Referees asked managers when it was convenient, and it was sometimes as much as twenty minutes before kick-off. That was ridiculous because it takes only seconds for a player to change his boots, and anyone seeking to gain an illegal advantage has plenty of time to make the switch once the dressing-room door has closed again.

That meant the operation was pointless, and thankfully the authorities amended this instruction by making it optional. It would be far more sensible for the referee to check the studs in the tunnel as the players were running out. Then no one could gain an unfair advantage, and there would still be time for anything the referee found offensive to be changed before the match started, although it would also be an effective deterrent if the match were to start without any offender who could not make the necessary switch in time for the kick-off.

Another grey area where a referee has to use his discretion is on the question of allowing a trainer on to treat an injured player. While no one could deny that some players, particularly some on the Continent, do feign injuries, a referee is treading on a tightrope if he sets himself up as the judge of whether a player is genuinely hurt or not.

They are not qualified to judge and it is probably the area about which they know least. It has also become a lot harder because trainers these days are invariably qualified, intelligent medical men compared with the sponge-and-bucket trainers of the old days.

When I finished as a player I qualified as a physiotherapist, and when I was trainer at Anfield I knew I could baffle referees with science if I could get on to the pitch. Half the time all I wanted to do was get on the pitch for coaching purposes – to get a point home to a player. Any excuse would do, and I remember one day at Newcastle chasing a dog round the pitch. I eventually caught it and carried it away – but not before I'd had a word with two or three players as we were trying to catch it. For all I knew the dog could have had rabies, but I had something important to point out to the players.

Often, too, the signs would go out from the dug-out for a player to go down injured after the next tackle, and as often as not it would be in order to speak to the referee while he hovered over us to prevent me coaching the player. I'd point out to the referee all the mistakes he was making and the things he was missing – even if he wasn't – to try to intimidate him into leaning our way.

I don't pretend I was ethically right in doing it, but it was part and parcel of my job and that of every trainer in the game. The late Les Cocker was an expert at it when he was Don Revie's right-hand man at Leeds. It was probably Billy Bremner's familiarity with the ploy under Les Cocker that once prompted him to run half the length of the pitch to 'listen in' while I was treating one of our players during a Liverpool–Leeds match.

Over the years you got to know which referees you could influence, but I will hold up my hand to the official – I seem to remember it was Clive James of York – for a decision he made before a cup-tie at Coventry one night. The night before there had been a heavy frost, and during the day half the pitch thawed while the other half remained frozen in the shadow of a stand. It was, as we say, a two-faced pitch, calling for studs on one side and rubber-soled boots on the other.

The game could well have been called off, with all the usual consequences of fixture congestion and the problem of finding a new date. But the referee made sure the game went ahead by tossing up for choice of ends in the dressing-room an hour before the game. It meant that both teams knew what footwear each of their players would need in the first half, and allowed time, not only for that to be arranged, but also for a half-time change of boots to be prepared.

That decision ensured there was no inconvenience to either the clubs, the players or the fans, many of whom had spent a lot of money travelling a long way, and he at least tried to get an evenly balanced match.

When conditions are bad, a lot of thought has to be given to whether an important match should be allowed to go on or not. Ice, snow and thick mud are a handicap to a good team and the game levels off to the advantage of the inferior team. Which is why I don't think managers should ever be consulted on whether a game should be played. It's always a fair bet that when they are consulted they will disagree. In the depths of winter it's an important part of a referee's job, and he needs assistance with it. It would be better, surely, for the assessor, who after all is supposed to be a former referee, to help in the decision.

Another area where a referee could be helped is at corners. He is supposed to do all he can to keep the game flowing, but how often you see it held up in such a situation because a defending player is fewer than ten yards from the ball at a corner. All it needs is a little line, only a few inches long, intersecting the goal-line exactly ten yards from the corner flag. Then there would be no argument about where a defender should be.

The question of encroachment at free-kicks is often a vexed problem, but referees often do not do enough to help themselves. A little common sense could often tell them how far ten yards is, just by using the pitch markings as a guide instead of the tedious pacing that some referees do. That quality is something that certain referees could do with a bit more of, because it is common sense and discretion that can help as much as anything else in improving standards.

I welcomed the raising of the retirement age to forty-eight, but I would still like to see it dispensed with altogether and the retirement of a referee left until he can no longer maintain his standards – something that can be judged by the assessors.

And there must still be a place in the game for retired referees. There is already a Referees' and Linesmen's Association, but it needs to have a stronger, more authoritative voice. Retired officials could play a big part here, just as they could at special courses for referees. While a classroom atmosphere is cool, calm and calculating, and far removed from actual match conditions, there are still many pointers and guide-lines which could be passed on from the wealth of experience gained by some of the top referees in controlling matches throughout the world.

At present they learn it the hard way in the non-league arena, and while that practical experience is good, a little help and guidance would not be a bad thing either. They could be advised on training, fitness, preparation, and ways to avoid unnecessary trouble, which is often caused by a referee's inexperience. And all of that would help towards uniformity, a raising of standards and an improvement in the game. And that's what we all want.

11 The Media Machine

When I succeeded Bill Shankly one of the areas of the job I was least equipped to handle was the media. Being in the background for thirty-five years even as a player before joining the training staff, meant I had little contact with the world of newspapers and the growing importance of radio and television.

Today, it's a massive industry, directly linked to football, and a manager must come to terms with it whatever his personal feelings. I thought I was getting a little long in the tooth to change my habits, and in my first season I found it particularly difficult dealing with the public relations side of the game.

Because of Liverpool's success I have appeared on television many times in the last few years, but I still don't feel comfortable about it and only agree to do so in the interests of the club and supporters.

What made it even harder was that Bill was a natural, with the gift of giving the perfect quote to satisfy the most demanding pressman. That was something he was born with – he didn't even have to work at it. For me it was just the opposite. I have never had Bill's turn of phrase, and if I'd tried to dream them up in advance it would have been cheating. So to the media in general, I think, I came across as a rather dull and cautious person.

Shrewd old Uncle Bob they called me, which I suspect was a kind way to overlook my shortcomings in their eyes. It's not intentional and I don't try to avoid the media but I know I'm not giving them the type of instant headlines they probably want, and certainly got with Bill.

Newspapers remind me of *Jaws* – they'll consume anything you've got and be back for more the next day. It's impossible to give them too much, but I think I'm more aware of their problems now, and certainly the Press corps on Merseyside, the people I deal with on a day-to-day basis, have come to understand how I operate. Sometimes there will be a good news story, but it's never been my policy to provoke the type of argument or row which papers thrive on.

Bill spoke his mind and often it was left to the discretion of the journalist to protect him. Over the years Bill got to know who to trust and who to be wary of. It's an old newspaper cliché that the best stories never get printed and I know a few sportswriters who have had plenty of those up their sleeves after a session with Bill.

But for me that first season was like a minefield. I knew I over-reacted to criticism, even felt it was implied when it probably was not, but it was all down to my own inexperience with the media. I don't think they realise their own strength. The public can be influenced by them to an enormous degree.

When I was a player it was so different. You could walk out of the dressing-room at Anfield after a game and there would be nobody waiting for you. Our manager at the time was George Kay, and he would leave the ground and drive down to the Liverpool Press Club for a game of snooker with the local reporter. And in that leisurely atmosphere they might discuss the game, and the journalist might, but not always, use a quote.

Today, you can't move in the Anfield corridors after a game. Press, radio, television, usually around fifty people are waiting to consume every word you utter, and there is usually one with a loaded question designed to provoke a storm in a teacup.

It has to be admitted that there is a lack of trust between football clubs and the media. Maybe the conflict of interests makes this inevitable, although I believe Liverpool is coping with it better than most. The value of publicity is something no club can afford to ignore and maybe we do have something to learn from the Americans in marketing the game. But there has to be give and take on both sides. Fortunately it's not as bad in this country as in other parts of Europe.

When we met Inter Milan in our first season in the European Cup the Italian Press whipped up a hate campaign of such proportions that you couldn't fail to feel the vibrations. All sorts of wild allegations, including one of drug-taking, were hurled at us when we went to Milan defending a 3-1 lead. Passions ran high and we felt the full brunt of it. We lost the game, but to this day there are still questions being asked about the refereeing decisions, something which has happened again on occasions when an Italian club has been involved. That was the media in its worst form and I'm just relieved that nothing like that occurs in England.

More than once I've crossed swords with Jimmy Hill, one of the most influential figures in the media in this country. I recognise he is an intelligent man with considerable knowledge of football gained as a player, manager, administrator and analyst. But I think it is wrong that someone with a vested interest should also be in such a powerful position to sway the opinions of millions of people on television every weekend and sometimes in midweek as well.

Jimmy Hill is managing director of Coventry City, has had soccer links with the Middle East and the United States and acts as the game's mouthpiece in the eyes of the public here on television.

He has access to around ten million soccer fans on *Match of the Day* – and that's considerably more than actually attend matches. And in that capacity he has been guilty of several misguided statements concerning my club. What he says about others is for them to comment on, but I won't be silent when I hear someone like Jimmy Hill informing the nation of where we have gone wrong, which was the case after our European Cup defeat in Tbilisi in 1979. He cited the transfer of Emlyn Hughes and absence of Steve Heighway as two important factors, overlooking that the previous season we had set a new points record of 68 for the First Division championship – under the old two-points for a win system – scoring more goals than anyone else and conceding an all time low of sixteen. And neither Emlyn nor Steve could be classed as regulars in that team.

Because Jimmy Hill is actively involved with another First Division club, the temptation is to criticise them – there is certainly plenty to go at if I had a mind to do so but I repeat, that's not my style.

On one occasion featuring a game between Coventry and

Liverpool, Jimmy Hill was also at fault. Graeme Souness was involved in an incident with a Coventry player, which resulted in the Coventry player being carried off. Within minutes, with the game still in progress, there was an announcement over the Coventry tannoy stating that the home player had been taken to hospital. At half time I walked to the dressing-rooms with Jimmy Hill, who was already suggesting the Coventry player had broken his leg before he had even checked.

As it happened, the injury was nowhere near as serious as that, but the crowd's emotions were inflamed and the hate was naturally directed at my team. I think such actions by people who should know better do nothing for the image of the game. I recognise that Jimmy Hill is steeped in football and has made a major contribution to the game at several levels, but I think it's wrong for one man to have so many irons in the fire.

The Press in England also adopt vastly different stances. I get the impression that journalists in London are always looking to knock clubs like Liverpool and Manchester United. I've lost count of the number of new championship contenders who are supposed to be emerging from London only for them to disappear and be promptly replaced by another one. Crystal Palace were hailed as the team of the eighties by the London Press, which is a ridiculous tag to put on any side. I don't recall the intelligent Terry Venables ever making such a claim about his team, when he was their manager.

Maybe the scribes in Fleet Street get tired of the trek to Anfield and Old Trafford and it's just a case of wanting some success a little nearer home. But Fleet Street houses the supposedly top sportswriters and there are times when their bias against us shows through.

I remember when we played our first European Cup Final and one national newspaper on the eve of the game ran a story saying the best team in Europe wasn't even playing – Juventus were the élite, according to that particular paper! I wonder if they would have run that story if Arsenal or Spurs had been in the European Cup Final?

In my time as Liverpool manager, there were several top soccer writers based in London who I have barely had a word with, simply because they have never bothered to come to see me at Anfield. I wonder if their sports editors were aware of that?

Many of the Number One men only come to Anfield half a dozen times a year because they are based in London. Now in my opinion it's impossible for them or anyone else to get to know enough about us unless they see us regularly in our own environment.

I appreciate a national paper has to send its staff all over the country to watch as many teams as possible but if they are going to write with any authority on what makes us tick - or more to the point what our weaknesses are - I don't see how they can do it unless they are completely familiar with the subject. I'm sure that's why some of the opinions expressed about Liverpool - particularly those which are factually incorrect - stem from a basic lack of knowledge of what is going on at Liverpool. Goodness knows, the doors are always open. We've nothing to hide, as many foreign journalists can confirm.

I accept that, human nature being what it is, we all like to hear a bit of scandal and in football terms that is interpreted as a shock transfer request or a behind-the-scenes row. We don't have many of those at Anfield, so the scribes have to look elsewhere for something to titillate the reader's palate.

But I'm sure there is also a need for the media and football to promote the good side of the game. It might not make for big headlines, which I'm told help to sell newspapers, but when all is said and done we are all making a living out of the sport and I think we have a duty to nurture and protect it.

I can never understand people in my profession who say things just for effect. It's as though they are obsessed by having their names in print as often as possible. Some of the quotes attributed to football managers have dismayed me, and I've often wondered why they have made such outbursts.

Take John Bond, for example. Here is a man who did a remarkable job for Norwich City and would have my undivided admiration for his achievements with a small club and a limited budget. But from time to time John saw fit to make outrageous claims about other clubs – and Liverpool is one which has been on the receiving end.

If you judged John Bond strictly as a football manager, his record at Norwich stood comparison with anyone's, simply because he competed against bigger and richer clubs and was frequently more successful.

But it seems he has a chip on his shoulder and has to shout the loudest to be heard because he still adopted that attitude when he joined Manchester City.

Occasionally I've fallen into the trap of responding to remarks from people like John. It's not something I enjoy, but there are times when you feel duty bound to defend the name of your own club, and the media of course are always the winners – they love every word of a row story.

But if we were all shouting the odds together, trying to get our names in print, I'm sure even the football-loving public would soon get sick of it.

Matt Busby enjoyed a good working relationship with the Press, yet he rarely engaged in anything controversial. I try to do the same, but I suspect there will always be a permanent unease between the game and the media. There are black sheep in every family, and that's why we often eye each other with suspicion.

In some countries the Press is more powerful than the game itself. When we played the Turkish side Trabzon, in the European Cup, a bizarre incident demonstrated that. As I mentioned in the European Cup chapter, we flew to Ankara and stayed overnight before taking an internal flight for the rest of the journey. When we touched down, the pressmen in our party were immediately surrounded by the Turkish sportswriters while the team and officials were ignored. Apparently, the Turks were asking if the British journalists would have any objection if the match kick-off was brought forward one hour.

The reason was to enable photographers to get their film of the game on a flight leaving for Istanbul soon after the game started. It never occurred to the Turkish Press to consult our club or Trabzon. In fact it seemed to be taken for granted that the referee and UEFA would have no objections if it was okay with the British newspapers!

As the game was scheduled for an early afternoon start we didn't want to bring it forward still further, but I've often wondered what would have happened if the British journalists hadn't told us of the 'arrangement'. Would we have been disqualified for turning up late for the new kick-off? If so, it would have cost us dearly, because we went on to win the Cup that season. And I wonder how the fans would have reacted if they had turned up and found the game already sixty minutes old?

At the same match the Turkish Press showed their power when one of our directors was 'removed' from his seat because he had mistakenly wandered into the press area. That was fair enough, except the Trabzon club had forgotten to cater for visiting directors and there wasn't a spare seat in the stadium, which could take only 13,000 spectators.

I'm sure many people in football will see the amusing side of this, as directors don't always enjoy the best of reputations, but whatever the British Press may think of them, I can't see them being pushed out of a press-box at home, especially when there is nowhere else to go. But apparently in Turkey, what the Press says goes.

I realise I'm not a journalist's dream, but there are many times when I have little or nothing to say about Liverpool. I won't invent stories, and if you have a winning team with no injury problems you can hardly be expected suddenly to become controversial.

We don't like to sing our own praises at Anfield. We let others do that while we try to keep the players' feet on the ground, which I suppose blocks another avenue for publicity. But what we try to do is make the media men welcome. We don't employ any stringent measures, our players are allowed to talk freely on the understanding they are responsible, and nowhere is off limits.

At Anfield the Press can go where they like and talk to anyone, as long as they don't abuse that facility. That's the policy of the club from top to bottom. The chairman and the general secretary are always available to answer their questions, and so am I. There are many media men from home and abroad who can testify that we are generous hosts, so I don't think we have too much to answer for in this department of the game. I know for a fact that the same policy does not apply at many of our big clubs, where the Press are treated less favourably.

In time, maybe, football managers will have to go on a public relations course before they are allowed to run a club. But when you have been around as long as I have, it's virtually impossible to change the habits of a lifetime.

I try to co-operate where I can, but I'm too long in the tooth to change into a tub-thumping extrovert now.

12 The Great Managers

Liverpool have suffered a number of defeats at the hands of Manchester United over the years. Two that stand out in my time as manager were the Wembley FA Cup Final defeat of 1977 that cost us the treble, and the semi-final defeat that halted our double bid two years later.

But there was an important loss off the field many years earlier. That's when the man I consider the greatest manager of all time took charge of Manchester United after being offered the chance to stay on at Liverpool as a coach. Unfortunately the intervention of the Second World War had something to do with it. Liverpool offered him a job as coach but eventually he took the chance to take over United – and the rest is history.

The record of Sir Matt Busby speaks for itself. He led United to five League championships, two Wembley FA Cup Final triumphs, and, of course, the realisation of a dream when they became the first English team to win the European Cup. But there was much more to it than that. There was the style with which his United teams played – and the character of the man, shown at its greatest when he and the club fought back after the tragedy of Munich.

Matt was the captain of Liverpool when I came down from the North-East to join them. In those days I think the younger players showed a lot more respect for the older men than they do now. We certainly had a lot of respect for Matt Busby. As the captain he was always available to help anybody. You could go to him any time and know that he would help and he would do it in a wonderful manner. He was well spoken and so very diplomatic.

When he took over as manager at United they said the same as they said when I took over at Liverpool: 'He's got a ready-made team and can't go wrong.'

True, the team he took over had a number of very good players who were around twenty-six or twenty-seven years old, and considered then to be in their prime. But the club and the ground were certainly not in their prime.

Old Trafford was little more than a waste ground after the wartime bombing, aimed at the nearby docks. United had little money to draw on. For a long time they used Maine Road, the ground of Manchester City, the club where Matt enjoyed so much success as a cultured Scottish wing-half.

But the marvellous success story soon started. He showed those qualities as a manager he had shown as a captain – a diplomat who would never get flustered. He also showed the depth of his knowledge of football and the ability to gather players of talent together.

He relied on skill. He was a strict disciplinarian, although he never had to wield the big stick to get this discipline. He wanted his skilful men to express themselves. He never tied them down to tactical orders.

Matt got Manchester United going so well that by 1948, the year they beat Blackpool in the final to win the FA Cup, they had a side that I rate as the best I ever played against. They talk about total football now, but this was one of the great sides that played total football then. It was his personality coming through.

And Matt had the foresight to start building another team, and when the young team came through they were blessed with the same skill as the old one. There's no doubt in my mind that but for the Munich tragedy that would have become the greatest team of all time.

Even then, and despite the fact that he was badly injured, he had the endurance to come back and do it all over again. He would be the first to give a lot of credit to his aides, particularly Jimmy Murphy.

Jimmy was very close to Matt – a different kind of man, aggressive, a real enthusiast. But he was the perfect foil and they made the perfect partnership. He provided a lot of the drive. Matt possibly sensed that Jimmy had something he didn't have himself, and I've no doubt that's why he picked him. Nobody's perfect, but Matt made himself as near perfect as any manager's been by taking Jimmy on to help him.

After all that Matt goes and produces another great team. First of all they won the FA Cup. Then two championships. And in 1968 they became the first English club to win the European Cup. That must have been a wonderfully satisfying experience, realising that he was the pioneer of European football as far as England were concerned.

United were the first English club to enter the European Cup in 1956 – and Matt took them in against the wishes of the football authorities in this country. The Munich crash happened when United were on their way back from a European Cup match in Belgrade.

When you think about it, it was only right that Manchester United under Matt Busby should be the first English club to win the trophy. And although he did it in the end with a team that was not as good as some of those he produced before they really did it his way. There were players of flair in that side like Bobby Charlton, George Best and Pat Crerand. There was also a great deal of character.

Matt as a player was cultured and methodical, precise and very deliberate in his distribution. That's the way he ruled as a manager. He didn't go around shouting the odds. He thought everything out. As a player he would probably have liked to have been more mobile. When he became a manager he looked for the balance. He got it with Jimmy Murphy.

Most managers are like that, I believe. They look for something that was lacking in their own game. Often the secret is to recognise this and to do something about it. Matt, along with all his other qualities knew what to do about it. And that was one of the factors that helped to make him the greatest.

It goes without saying that Bill Shankly, another Scottish wing-half but so different to Matt in many ways, must be rated among the greatest of managers. Because he was so important to me and Liverpool and we were closely linked for fifteen years, I have gone into much greater detail about Bill in another chapter.

Like so many of the men I name among the great managers he was a playing contemporary of mine. I remember him as a hard, enthusiastic wing-half with Preston who never knew he was beaten. I like to think I played the game the same way myself.

Bill brought this tremendous enthusiasm to his management. This and his dedication were without doubt his greatest strengths. He was a fitness fanatic and I think this always showed in every team he managed, from his start at Carlisle to his great days at the top with Liverpool.

He liked enthusiastic men around him and really couldn't bear the quieter types. He had the ability to get all those who were connected with him, the backroom staff, players, everyone, to be like him. You had to eat, live and sleep football. You had to be prepared to think and talk about nothing else. And Bill's way was certainly the right way for him and Liverpool as the results proved.

Don Revie was for ten years Bill's great rival. But although Leeds and Liverpool were often locked in battle for the game's top honours the relationship between the clubs was always good.

Like so many managers I felt Don looked for something in his own teams that he did not have as a player. They seem to be after things that were not in their own game. Don was not an aggressive player. Leeds under him were always an aggressive, competitive team.

Leeds were in danger of relegation from the Second Division when he took over. He guided them to honours they'd hardly dared to dream about at Elland Road - two League titles, as well as FA Cup, League Cup and Fairs Cup triumphs.

He was very thorough, a stickler for detail. He was among the most tactically-minded of all managers. If there was a flaw it was possibly in the tendency to indulge in gamesmanship. But Don Revie and Leeds United commanded tremendous respect from Liverpool.

Like Matt, Don probably recognised what he lacked in his own make-up. As a player, remembered for the Revie Plan at Manchester City when he operated as a deep-lying centre-forward, he was the thoughtful type. As a manager he took on a lieutenant who was different - Les Cocker. Don had a quiet way with him,

Les was openly enthusiastic about everything. He provided the balance.

Sir Alf Ramsey must also go down among the greats. He was an excellent manager. He placed great importance on teamwork. He would leave a player everyone was crying out for out of his side if he felt that another player, even one who didn't have the popular support, would be more effective for the team.

He felt a hard man in the side was an essential. He had one in more or less every team he managed. Nobby Stiles was a typical example of this policy in his England team that won the World Cup – a case of not having the most elegant but the most effective.

In many ways he was of the same mind as me. He felt that possession was the important thing. He laid down that it was hard enough to get the ball in the first place so your distribution had to be of the highest quality to make sure you didn't give it away.

Don Revie approached it the same way. Matt Busby was probably prepared to let the flair of his side speak for him and take more chances.

Alf was accused of producing the wingless wonders because England won the World Cup without a recognised winger. But I know that if he felt he had a winger who was good enough he would have played him. Basically we all would.

They say he set the pattern that most people followed and that's why there aren't many wingers today. But in every game you see there are players going up the wings, even if we don't call them wingers.

Alf laid emphasis on the teamwork and control, particularly in the passing ability of the side. He did great work as a manager. He proved his worth as a club manager with his successes at Ipswich. He took a club out of the backwoods of football and set the pattern for them. They've kept going since he left, but he was the architect.

He won the World Cup with England, a tremendous achievement. He was acclaimed, then crucified. But he must be one of the all time greats.

Alf was never really associated with one particular partner or assistant, as so many other managers. Perhaps he did not feel the need to have the opposite type around to balance him. He seemed well-balanced enough himself. He was the first manager to really produce a successful team from East Anglia and that probably provided the confidence for him to make his own way.

But, as I've pointed out with Nobby Stiles as the example, he looked for something in his teams that was lacking in his own game. As a player he was immaculate in his approach. He could possibly have been a bit more aggressive and mobile. He was always calm, would never get ruffled. He was very accurate in his own play and as a manager he demanded accuracy from his players. He was never flashy and preferred a fairly simplified type of game. That showed in his teams – and they were good, effective teams.

Stan Cullis was another manager whose record spoke volumes for him. Wolves won League titles and FA Cups under him. They also brought us some early exciting experiences of European football. He was a very excitable person and this showed both in his play and later in his management.

As a player he was strong and gifted, particularly for a centre-half of those days. He was also a good leader, setting an example to his men on the field. He was a great competitor and I vividly remember his last match as a player, which must have been just about the biggest disappointment of his life.

It was at Molineux against Liverpool, and if Wolves won it they would take the League title, a marvellous climax to a great career. I was injured and had to sit it out. Liverpool won 2–1 and eventually became champions. Wolves, who had been nine points ahead of us with only seven games to play, finished third.

Stan was the kind of man who would never ask anyone to do something he couldn't do himself. He was steeped in the Wolves tradition. His teams were masters of the long-ball game. I believe that Wolves might have stayed successful for longer if Stan had had a partner or an assistant to provide the balance, possibly to point out that the type of game that had brought them so much success needed modifying.

At one time they said the same about Liverpool – that you always knew how we would play. But we changed our style. If Stan had changed the Wolves style a little bit things might have worked out differently for him and the club. I remember going down to watch one of the early European Cup games against Barcelona. The Spaniards certainly knew what to do with that style. They riddled Wolves with their possession play. They won 5–2 and I felt that highlighted the need for some modifications.

Of course, you cannot change things overnight and Wolves had been very successful. Everything was racy, speculative and exciting. They were the best exponents of that type of game. It would be interesting if we could turn the clock back and see what would have happened if they had been prepared to try something a bit different.

After Stan finished as a manager I thought he should have been used by the FA on disciplinary committees. He had been captain of Wolves and England. He'd been a successful manager. He was fair-minded and he had integrity. There was never anything devious in his outlook to football. I felt this type of person could help the disciplinary system to work better.

Joe Mercer came from the same neck of the woods as Stan – Ellesmere Port – and was of the same generation. He's always been a great character and he proved himself one of the great managers, too. Like Stan, I have a vivid memory of Joe's last game as a player. I didn't play in it but I watched it and Joe, then Arsenal's captain, broke his leg in an accidental collision with a team-mate.

Probably he was influenced by the great Everton side when he was a youngster at Goodison Park. Certainly in football, as player and manager, his attitude reflected his outlook on life. He always looked for flair. He wanted to entertain. That showed through most of all as a manager when he went to Manchester City and had that wonderful partnership with Malcolm Allison and in the short period of time when he was in charge of the England team.

City were in the Second Division when Joe and Malcolm came together at Maine Road. But in five years they rose to carry off the League title and the FA, League and European Cup Winners' Cups. And they did it in exciting, swashbuckling fashion. It was a pity that partnership broke up. Both men had so much to offer. There was Joe's wise counsel and Malcolm's coaching ability. It seemed the perfect partnership and when it broke up I don't think it was Joe's doing.

On the surface Joe had a carefree manner – but he was totally committed to the game and at one time, when he was in charge of Aston Villa this commitment made him ill. He was a lover of skill and probably enjoyed himself most as a manager and showed his flair when he was in charge of the England team. It was only a short period, between Sir Alf Ramsey's departure and Don Revie's appointment, but I'm sure the players enjoyed playing under Joe. We certainly enjoyed watching his teams then – and they got results.

One of my favourite stories that shatters the myth about great half-time team talks comes from Joe. It was a match at Villa Park against Liverpool. We were three up at half time and giving Villa a real hiding. They fought back for a 4–4 draw and the next day the papers were full of stories about Mercer's magic in his half-time talk. There was no magic, he told us. He'd been so upset he'd hardly been able to say a thing and had kicked the tea urn in disgust.

Harry Catterick was a player with Joe at Everton for a while, and for 10 years he was Bill Shankly's great managerial rival on Merseyside. Like so many managers he seemed to look for qualities in players that he lacked himself. I played against him a few times. When he arrived at Everton as a young centre-forward he knew he had a fight on his hands. Two of the other centre-forwards on the books were Dixie Dean and Tommy Lawton. But Harry had a go.

He was an aggressive player, a hard worker who set out to worry the opposition all the time. In the modern game he could have been the ideal foil for a skilful partner. In the role of a twin striker he could have provided the balance for the other type. The skilful partner might have helped Harry to bring out more skill from his own game.

As a manager Harry served a valuable apprenticeship at Crewe and then Rochdale – where Joe Fagan, who has been so closely linked with me at Liverpool, was his trainer. Then he took over at Sheffield Wednesday and did an excellent job, lifting them into the runners-up spot behind the great Spurs double team.

Then he was given the Everton job and in 1963 guided the club to their first League title since 1939. Later they won the FA Cup, in 1966, and the championship again, in 1970, under him.

He went for a skilful team of ball players, and he certainly got it with that 1970 side which had at the heart that wonderful midfield trio of Alan Ball, Howard Kendall and Colin Harvey. It was one of Everton's greatest sides and it must have given him great satisfaction. It was a pity that team did not stay together longer. I don't know why, but it broke up quicker than it should have.

During Bill Shankly's reign at Anfield another of his great rivals was Bill Nicholson at Tottenham. Bill went down to London to join Spurs from Scarborough shortly before I left the North-East to join Liverpool.

He was a good strong wing-half who helped Spurs to win the championships of the Second and First Divisions in successive seasons and also played for England – a team-mate of Alf Ramsey. But he was different from Alf as a player and as a manager in a number of ways.

As a player he was stronger, and he was basically equipped to deal with any situation. As a manager he probably looked for more flair from his players than Alf – again looking for something that was not in his own game.

He was blessed with a number of fine individual players when he took over as manager of Tottenham but he moulded them into a great side. He looked first for individual qualities and then organised the team. He certainly achieved his objective. The side that did the League championship-FA Cup double in 1961 and went on to win the FA Cup again the following season possessed outstanding qualities. It rivalled the best that Britain has produced. And under Bill Nicholson Spurs went on to produce more attractive sides who won more trophies for them both in Europe and in this country.

Jock Stein was a manager few of us down in England had heard of until he achieved his outstanding successes with Celtic. But he showed his qualities early on with Dunfermline. Sound and knowledgeable, he made sure his teams played to their strengths. The Scots like to attack. It's a trait in their game. Jock loved his men and he gave them the freedom to go out and do what they liked doing best.

The Celtic team that made history by bringing the European Cup back to Britain for the first time in 1967 was among the best we've ever had in these Islands. Inter-Milan, the side they beat in that memorable Lisbon final, were no mean performers. They were much more experienced campaigners than Jock's boys and at times they could put up the kind of defensive barrier that was almost impossible to break down. But Celtic went out and did it in magnificent fashion.

There have been those who played down Jock's achievements by saying Celtic would not have won so much if they played in a more competitive League. But nine successive titles is magnificent in any country. And Jock's teams did it in an adventurous way. They were never tied down to defence. They always went out to attack the opposition. Jock must rank very high in any list of great managers.

Inevitably, I hear the question: What about Cloughie? I believe it is impossible to say where Brian Clough and his partner, Peter Taylor, figured in the managerial honours list. Whatever they achieved together - and it was plenty - there could still be more successes to come.

They typified the perfect partnership, with one acting as foil for the other. Sometimes I thought they did things between themselves to get the rebound off the other. They seemed like two people who would not sit in the same room. It was like an Agatha Christie mystery but they sparked each other off and brought each other out.

They had so much success together that it is very interesting to see them operate apart. But I always felt it had to be Brian and Peter together. They have good tactical knowledge and the basis of their success, wherever it's been achieved, has been teamwork. Like Liverpool, their requirements for a side are simple. There's nothing complicated about their type of game. Surely, there's a message there for others.

Brian's whole personality, I believe, is made for football today. There are certain things about the modern game that are foreign to me. I'm not saying they should not be in the game. They're just not me – but they are Brian.

There's something about him I've never been able to fathom out. I'll have to ask him about it one day. One of the things he takes very seriously is the smartness of players' dress, and yet he himself can turn up on occasions in a tracksuit and carrying a squash racket. It mystifies me.

I remember him as a player who simply loved to score goals. He had this self-confidence and that's obviously been very important to him. Yet as a manager he always insisted on the organisation in his teams, with the emphasis on a tight defence. I wonder how Clough the manager would have got on with Clough the player.

Having said that, he's certainly got the secret of success and knows how to get the best out of his men on the field. He's been successful at every level. You can't hold the Leeds episode against him, for he wasn't really given a chance there. He felt he had to do something to change things and he wasn't given time. In a few weeks he was out.

All the managers I've discussed so far were rivals of Bill Shankly or me. But there's another one, not so well remembered by the general public now, who had an influence on me.

George Kay was the manager who signed me for Liverpool from Bishop Auckland. He had played for West Ham in that first Wembley FA Cup Final against Bolton. At Liverpool he built a very good side.

The manager's job has changed a lot in my forty-odd years in the game. There weren't many tracksuit types around when I started. George was one of the old school in that respect. But he was very knowledgeable – not a tactical genius, but sound and sensible.

He was totally committed to the game. His only diversion seemed to be to play snooker at the Press Club. His commonsense outlook left a big impression on me.

Since George's day, of course, there have been great changes. Not least has been the spread of European football, and here I have come across a number of other great managers, although on the Continent their title is coach.

One of the first we came across was Helenio Herrera, of Inter-Milan. He was never the most popular of coaches, particularly on Merseyside where Inter's semi-final defeat of Liverpool in the European Cup in 1965 still rankles. But he was certainly made for the Italian type of game. He played to his team's strengths, which were based on very strong defence. Few sides were capable of breaking them down, although in the first leg of our controversial semi-final at Anfield we had him holding his head in his hands as we attacked them and won 3–1. And in 1967, in the Lisbon final, Celtic's positive play also shattered them.

Rinus Michels was another adversary of our early European days. Ajax, then an unknown quantity outside Holland, shattered us in the European Cup in 1966. Michels was a powerful influence on both Ajax and the successful Dutch national team. He was very confident in his approach and he believed in total football. He was probably fortunate that in his great teams he had Johann Cruyff as his general out on the pitch.

Through the years we've had many keen tussles in European competition with the West Germans, and two of their coaches, Hennes Weisweiler and Udo Lattek, are high on my list.

Weisweiler was really the architect of Borussia Moenchengladbach. He made them a respected force in football throughout the world. And although he was also associated with other successful clubs I would think the football of Borussia must have given him the greatest pleasure. They were what I call a working-class club. Their approach was similar to ours in that all their players were prepared to work for each other.

Under the influence of Weisweiler they came together with a good mixture of home-produced youngsters and some outstanding Scandinavians. I remember playing them in the 1973 UEFA Cup Final. We were very thankful for our 3–0 lead from the first leg, although for a while we feared that might not prove enough. For an hour they played some marvellous football. I don't know why he left, but I've always felt he must have felt very sad to leave such a team.

Later we came across him again. He was in charge of Barcelona when we met them in the 1976 UEFA Cup semi-final. Cruyff, who had proved invaluable to Michels, possibly proved his downfall. I know that when we won the first leg over there the atmosphere was not very good, and Weisweiler departed soon afterwards.

But he was very sound, knowledgeable and a good tactician, and I will always associate him with that fine team at Borussia Moenchengladbach.

Lattek followed Weisweiler at Borussia. He had already enjoyed great success with Bayern Munich, taking them to two European Cup triumphs. He had more success with Borussia. I always think of him as a typical German coach – very thorough.

Both men must have been greatly influenced by Helmut Schoen, the great West German national team coach. In many ways Schoen was like Matt Busby, a diplomat who knew the game from A to Z.

In the European Cup in 1973 we came up against a Yugoslav coach who certainly gained our respect. Miljan Miljanic guided Red Star Belgrade to a rare double over us. His side were one of the few to beat us in both legs of a European tie. He knew the game and he was also likeable. He had a pleasant, friendly approach and was very well liked throughout football.

Ernst Happel, of Bruges, was a different kettle of fish. I don't know whether he was arrogant, carefree or what. He certainly wouldn't be pushed around, however, and he was certainly a good coach. We met the Belgian side in two finals – the 1976 UEFA Cup and the 1978 European Cup.

He did his homework and made it very difficult for us. In fact in that UEFA Cup Final it looked as if he had made it impossible for us when Bruges came out and took an early 2–0 lead in the first leg at Anfield. We eventually won the trophy on a 4–3 aggregate.

Then at Wembley in the European Cup Final Bruges had a number of injury problems, but Happel's tactics made sure that they made it very difficult for us.

Another man who left a big impression was the Russian Nadari Akhalkatsi, who was in charge of Dynamo Tbilisi when they knocked us out of the European Cup in 1979. I had a long chat with him over a drink at Anfield when he came over to watch us before the first leg. He came around to our hotel for another chat after the second leg in Tbilisi and he was at the airport to see us off the next day. He was a very pleasant fellow.

His team had players with flair and he organised them to bring out their best. He did his homework on us, going into tiny details. We weren't at our best at the time, but he certainly did his job and had a lot to do with their win. Perhaps they thought they'd done the hard part and didn't go into so much detail for their meetings with Hamburg in the next round, for they lost both legs. But still I think we are going to hear a lot about him, possibly in connection with the Russian national team.

Back in England, Ron Saunders was around as a leading rival for many of my managerial years. He had his problems, particularly at Aston Villa, but I said long before he guided them to the title in 1981 that if they left him to do the job his way he would do it well.

I respect him as a good, honest man. He likes his pound of flesh all along the line and he doesn't suffer fools gladly. When a board appoints a Ron Saunders to be manager of their club they should have an idea of his assets. They shouldn't try to take those assets away from him.

It was no surprise to me that he built the Villa side the way he did and got them playing his way to win the championship. It was a pity he left soon after that title triumph at Villa Park. He had problems at Norwich and Manchester City, too, and while I respect him for what he is I also know there are times when you have to soft pedal a bit. You have to know when to bend like a branch in the wind.

Bobby Robson deserves a tremendous amount of credit for a terrific job of work at Ipswich. I always felt that in that part of the world, with the farming character, it was not the best place to get the enthusiasm and excitement for football. They're less excitable than city people. But he built some very good teams who played exciting football. He must have had an awful lot going for him and an awful lot of qualities. Now he has followed the same route from that outpost to the England manager's job that Sir Alf took years earlier.

Lawrie McMenemy, another North-Easterner, has done a wonderful job at Southampton, producing a successful side to compete with the big clubs in a difficult football area. He likes sides that play entertaining football – and his record for buying players must be one of the secrets of his success. Often the players he bought were getting on in years; some might argue they were too old. But by and large they paid their way and played entertaining football. That's got to be good.

Keith Burkinshaw surprised many people by the way he came to the top with Spurs. I like to think the board at White Hart Lane recognised something in him I always thought he had. Even though they were relegated they kept their faith in him and he kept his faith in the Spurs way of playing football. He's followed on the great lines of Bill Nicholson.

He was a reserve player at Liverpool when I was in charge of the second team. He was a dour type, but very dependable and honest in his work. He wouldn't cheat at anything. He gave a lot of thought to the game and it was no surprise to me that after leaving us to join Joe Harvey at Workington he took an interest in coaching and eventually became a top manager.

Of course, at Liverpool we took great pleasure in the success at Swansea of another Anfield 'old boy', John Toshack. It was an incredible achievement to take a side from the Fourth Division to the First in four years – far easier said than done. It showed an excellent knowledge of the game.

First of all he took experienced players from us and used them until he felt the moment was right for readjustment. He kept doing that through the divisions, getting the right quality to succeed in that standard of football. That's excellent management.

13 The Leaving of Liverpool

I reached my decision to bow out as Liverpool manager as a new generation of Anfield players were sweeping towards the 1982 championship and League Cup double. The time had come to think seriously about relinquishing the reins. And two thoughts were uppermost in my mind. The first was that young players had broken through into the team to provide a foundation to pass on to my successor. The second was that I had become aware of growing speculation amongst our supporters and the general public about when I was going to retire. That can only have an unsettling effect, and you cannot ignore it. They were starting to ask similar questions before Bill Shankly dropped the bombshell of his retirement and it is frustrating for both parties – me and the fans.

So I came to the conclusion that it was time for a new manager, and I envisaged my successor being one of these three: Joe Fagan, Ronnie Moran or Roy Evans. The club had to give one of them a chance, because who is to say who will make a manager or who won't? Who was to say whether I would succeed when I followed Bill in 1974? At the same time, Liverpool have expressed a keenness for me to stay on in some form of advisory capacity – which could be difficult.

The business of offering advice is fraught with problems. It would never have worked, for instance, if Bill had stayed in that capacity when I took over from him. Bill didn't give advice. He gave orders. But advice, by its very nature, must be something other people can take or leave. I would have thought Sir Matt

Busby was the ideal person to fill such a role. Yet even he came in for some stick for allegedly showing his hand after retiring as Manchester United manager to become general manager and, later, a director. But knowing Matt as I do, and with the respect I have for him, I doubt if that criticism was valid. It does, though, underline the pitfalls of being 'pushed upstairs'.

Whatever happens, leaving the manager's chair at Anfield is going to be a massive wrench for me. Football and Liverpool have been my life, a drug I've been hooked on.

My prime consideration when I was mulling over the prospect of retirement was the team my successor would inherit. The way youngsters like Ronnie Whelan and Ian Rush have come through, helping to win two trophies in their first season at the top level, has influenced me greatly. Of course there are seasoned campaigners in the squad, as, inevitably, there always will be. But there is plenty of talent to build on for the future. Players like Mark Lawrenson, Sammy Lee, Craig Johnston, Bruce Grobbelaar, as well as Whelan and Rush, should have many years ahead of them – barring injuries, for which nobody can legislate.

My successor, all being well, will take over a team of which about half the players have still to reach their peak. That is a fair proportion, and more than I was left with when I succeeded Bill. Even though we had won the 1974 FA Cup a couple of months before his retirement, there was a bit of age in the squad and several players who had loyally served the club for years, such as Chris Lawler, Tommy Smith and Ian Callaghan. It is some indication of the standards Liverpool had already set themselves, never mind others, that my first season in charge was classed as failure – and we finished second in the First Division!

So there is no doubt that whoever takes over from me is going to have a job on his plate, just as I had following Bill. Liverpool expect success, and the rest of football and the public also expect us to be successful. That is something the whole club has to live with and the manager can never forget.

We have a marvellous backroom team at Anfield who share the work-load wonderfully well. No club has a more able and closely-knit staff than ours. The Anfield 'boot-room' has become legendary, and we have a full and frank exchange of views in there in a leisurely atmosphere every Sunday morning. It's just like popping down to the local. But despite all that, there are times when the manager has to stand alone and take a decision. Sometimes you can deliberate on them for days, even weeks. But others have to be snap decisions, made spontaneously when the game is under way. If you don't possess that spark, that feeling deep inside for the game, that I have never lost and Bill Shankly never lost, your ability to make those decisions is impaired.

Two of the decisions I look back on with most satisfaction both concern substitutions ... yet they were done in totally different circumstances for totally different reasons.

Before our 1981 European Cup semi-final second leg with Bayern in Munich – for which we had been written off in many quarters after a goal-less draw in the first leg at Anfield – the official UEFA observer at the game alerted me to something I believe played an enormous part in helping us knock out the West Germans and go on to win the trophy by beating Real Madrid in Paris. For a start, it is uncommon for UEFA's man to speak the language of both competing clubs. But when he started asking questions about Howard Gayle, one of our substitutes, it was something that had never happened before in all our years in Europe.

'Who is this?' he asked, as if we were including an ineligible player in our squad. I knew for certain that if *he* had raised a query about Gayle, the Germans would be wondering about him too. Such is the efficiency and planning of most Continental clubs, and particularly the Germans, that Gayle was the only player they knew nothing about. Probably, they could have recited the rest of our squad off by heart with every player's role and what they thought were his strengths and weaknesses. But not Gayle. He provided the element of the unknown.

That fact became very important after only six minutes of the game when we suffered the shattering blow of losing Kenny Dalglish with an ankle ligament injury after a bad tackle by Calle Del'Haye. But for the query over Howard Gayle raised by the UEFA observer, I would have sent on Ian Rush to replace Kenny.

But true to the message of my favourite poem, Rudyard Kipling's 'If', I tried to keep a cool head and made the muck or nettles decision to send on Gayle.

I suspected and hoped that move would unsettle the Germans and send their planning haywire. That's exactly what happened. He ran Bayern ragged with his pace, and eventually tired himself so much that he started to retaliate and, in turn, had to be replaced by Jimmy Case. But Ray Kennedy's goal in a 1–1 draw took us through to the final on the away goal rule.

Just as I had spotted that Gayle was reacting to the effects of exhaustion in Munich – because as a general rule only tired players retaliate against opponents – I had to bring off Craig Johnston in a League game against Sunderland for exactly the opposite reason. He was too lively.

That game against Sunderland came just three days after we had gone out of the European Cup to CSKA Sofia in Bulgaria, owing to some of the strangest refereeing decisions I have ever seen, from Austrian official Franz Woehrer. The players, naturally, were mentally turned over by the experience, and as we had the championship in our sights, a win that day was paramount and the manner of it secondary. The team could not have withstood another disappointment very easily.

Because Sunderland were next to bottom we were expected to trounce them. But the way they were fighting to stave off relegation – they eventually succeeded in doing so – I could see signs that they were threatening to snatch a draw after we had gone ahead through an early goal from Ian Rush. If we had dropped two points then it could have cost us the title, and my job was to try to ensure that we held our lead and won the game.

Craig was the liveliest player on the field, but knowing the mental state of the rest of our lads, that was a threat in itself and he could have stretched them too far. It's like being at sea in a fog. The convoy must keep together so that no vessel becomes isolated or exposed. A football team is just the same. When there is danger you close ranks.

So I took Craig off and sent on David Johnson for the last twenty minutes, only to receive a dog's abuse from a handful –

and I stress a handful – of spectators. I was accused of being stupid for taking him off. But I would rate that decision one of the key factors in our championship success.

I have been with Liverpool since 1939, and nobody knows the Anfield supporters better than me. They have always liked tearaway players with an 'up and at 'em' style, a dash of humour and sense of adventure. The perfect example is the contrast in their response to the two Kennedys – Alan and Ray. Alan, a colourful character they have nicknamed 'Barney Rubble', has been far more popular with our fans than Ray was. And Ray was a sophisticated, knowledgeable player who did a tremendous job for us. Similarly, when I was playing they responded to my tigerish tackling and robust style more than they did to the elegance of Phil Taylor, a superb distributor of the ball.

The Liverpool crowd will always make allowances for a player as long as he's seen to be a trier. And while some players have obvious skill and effort – Billy Liddell and Kenny Dalglish are classic examples – many who have been triers in a different and not so obvious way have not been appreciated as much as they should have been. And when it comes to decisions such as the substitution of Craig Johnston against Sunderland I just wish they would try to look for an explanation before jumping in to criticise.

Generally, of course, Liverpool supporters are renowned for the encouragement they give the team, and they are part of the legend of the club. I remember Bill Shankly being quite upset one day that they'd stopped singing 'You'll Never Walk Alone' too soon. 'They should have given us another verse, Bob,' he said to me. And he wasn't joking.

I think that the sheer volume of European football served up at Anfield since 1964 has had an effect on our fans. They are knowledgeable about Continental football and have become selective in the matches they watch. And if we are playing what they rate as inferior opposition they tend to pre-judge games. That can lead to frustration on the terraces that spills over on to the field and does the players no favours.

The mental condition of players is just as vital as the physical. That was one of the reasons why I stripped Phil Thompson of the

Liverpool captaincy midway through the 1981–82 season. The earlier uncertainty over whether England were going to qualify for the World Cup Finals had put our three England men – Thompson, Terry McDermott and Phil Neal – mentally on the floor. Thompson was struggling to do his own centre-back job, never mind carry the extra responsibility of being captain, which always has to override individual performances. For his own good I took the captaincy off him and gave it to Graeme Souness.

I joked once that Graeme tosses up before kick off with a gold-plated credit card. What I was referring to was that touch of arrogance that a captain should have. Whereas Phil's loss of confidence affected both his form and his captaincy, Graeme can still show commanding leadership even if his own game is off the boil.

The mental demands of the game also have a marked effect on young players, which is why our 1982 championship win was all the more remarkable, with six of the squad winning their first title medals. Ever since Arsenal turfed Cliff 'Boy' Bastin into their First Division team at the age of seventeen, and he went on to win every honour in the game before his twenty-first birthday, people have trotted out the old cliché, 'If he's good enough, he's old enough.' What they overlook is the number of games top clubs face today, and the mental pressures which hit a youngster more than an experienced player. You can't be right physically if you are mentally out of tune, and the great risk is of a young player over-stretching himself and sustaining a chronic injury that will blight him for the rest of his career.

Ronnie Whelan and Ian Rush performed excellently to win a championship medal in their first season in the First Division at the age of twenty. Both of them played key roles in the team's dream run from the turn of the year. Yet they were both beginning to feel the pinch at the end of the season, even though neither of them had been in the team at the start of it. You have to nurse youngsters through, keeping an alert eye for any signs of tiredness, and give them a break when you feel they need one.

We do not as a general rule come down like a ton of bricks on players after a bad result or let them go on a cruise after a good one. That is one of the broad principles of Liverpool, and if they are ignored I don't know how long the success will continue.

The club has a touch of communism – in the strictly non-political sense. Nobody at Liverpool tries to hog the limelight. There is a lack of conceit, no false pride and, with it, a lack of fear. There is a passion within the club, even among the tea ladies and the cleaners. Individual titles are not very important at Liverpool because there is still a family atmosphere about the place. If I'm walking down a corridor and see a bit of dust on the floor I'll find a brush and sweep it up myself if one of the cleaners isn't around. That may be an extreme example, but nobody at Anfield will let a job remain undone – even somebody else's – if they can possibly do it themselves. We try never to put off until tomorrow what we can do today.

Football is *still* only a game at Liverpool, despite our huge successes. The club's approach has been the same for years . . . the enthusiasm, the will to win yet enjoy it, and keeping the right habits. Something I might have said once about treatment for a certain injury may come back to me ages later from Joe Fagan or Ronnie Moran. You can never do the right thing too often.

Everyone who works for Liverpool FC believes it is important to uphold the image of the club, and it's amazing how even the most egotistical players who have arrived have been infected by the atmosphere and changed by it.

At Liverpool we believe that football is not a complicated game, and we've probably cashed in on other people who do complicate it. We've bought players who were good when they arrived but still found room to develop and improve. Great players like Kenny Dalglish and Graeme Souness have become better for coming to Anfield, because we like to give them room to expand their talents.

What we look for in a player is character and the raw material. If we sign him we concentrate on drawing out his assets. And while we try to counter any weaknesses in his game, we don't harp on about what he can't do, because the perfect player has never been born.

Phil Neal, for example, was there for any club to see, playing Fourth Division football for Northampton. Our chief scout Geoff

Twentyman alerted us to Phil because we were looking for back four cover. Phil was my first signing, and the £60,000 we paid for him was hardly an outrageous fee, even though Tommy McAnearney said that Aldershot were going to sign him for £10,000. That was in 1974, and even after his amazing consistency has seen Phil set new appearance records for Liverpool and win a host of England caps, people still snipe that he can't defend. Well, he must have been doing something right both for me and England over those years! Phil had the basic qualities we always look for and perhaps other clubs don't.

I also believe there is a kind of 'mafia' in the game, with scouts huddled in a corner agreeing that a certain player can or can't do this, that or the other. They just jump on the bandwagon. One man condemns a player and others follow, or else they all hail him as a great player.

Football is riddled with so many fancy ideas and long words these days that you need a dictionary as well as football boots and a ball. While we at Liverpool say we believe it is a simple game, and keep the same habits year after year, other people pay lip service and agree. But invariably they don't try to put it into practice. They would rather be expounding some high-falutin' theory. You would think they were talking about burglars when they refer to 'getting in around the back', or electricians when the words 'positive' and 'negative' are bandied about. One player at a coaching course was said to 'lack environmental sense'. What on earth does that mean in football terms? Football is still a working-class game, but a certain element within it try to make it something it isn't.

I'm sure whoever follows me at Liverpool will also follow the pattern which has been laid down at the club. The present has to look after itself, and you just hope you are prepared for it – but we learn from the past and always look and plan ahead to the finest detail if at all possible.

As I look ahead and contemplate life without being manager of Liverpool – and my wife Jessie has warned me what an upheaval it's going to be for me – I also reflect on three previous occasions when I pondered my future with the club.

The first time was in 1950, when I was left out of Liverpool's side to play Arsenal in the FA Cup Final. I had scored one of the goals that beat Everton in the semi-final at Maine Road, and I was shattered not to make the final. I was also led into temptation by a Sunday newspaper to write a signed article. I declined the offer to do any muck-raking, but when I got to Wembley that day I couldn't even bear to look at our manager George Kay. With twelve men for eleven positions in the days before substitutes, he opted for Bill Jones to play in my left-half position alongside his England colleague Laurie Hughes. But when George Kay got on the coach after the game - which we lost 2-0 - I could see that he had received no pleasure from leaving me out of the team, even though we didn't talk about it. The whole experience was something I've never forgotten and I've faced similar situations as a manager myself. The irony was that the season after that final I made the most first-team appearances by playing in forty-one of the forty-two League games.

Four years after that bitter Wembley disappointment, I found myself at the crossroads again when I was given a free transfer, along with Bill Jones, Phil Taylor and Eddie Spicer, and I was contemplating returning to my old job as a bricklayer. But I had taken a correspondence course in physiotherapy, because I'd fancied the idea of a trainer's job (a coach in those days was something you rode in).

Fortunately for me, Liverpool director T. V. Williams, later chairman and president of the club, fixed me up with a job on the Anfield staff under the management of Don Welsh, who had succeeded George Kay. I gained valuable experience working with the reserve team - guiding them to the club's first ever Central League title - and the youth team, before becoming assistant to manager Phil Taylor after he had taken over from Don. But when Reuben Bennett was brought down from Scotland early in 1959, the Liverpool futures of both myself and Phil seemed in doubt, and I said to him that we would have to make a stand. A local journalist drafted a letter on our behalf, which we handed to the club. But while, sadly, it signalled the end of Phil's career at Anfield, I was assured I would be kept on. And in

December of that same year Bill Shankly arrived from Huddersfield to start something that is still rolling merrily along more than two decades later.

I only hope the momentum of success shows no sign of slowing for the next incumbent of the manager's desk in that little, window-less room at Anfield.